"In a world of dime-a-dozen crime stories, Zacharias unearths one like no other I've read. This exhaustively researched book is deep in its linking of two murders to nature as well as nurture, wide in its piecing together thousands of pieces to create a single puzzle, and chilling in its reminder that evil, unfortunately, abides. The result is a book that will make you reconsider the insidiousness of murder in an all-new way."

—Bob Welch, author of *Boy in the Mirror: An Athletic Director's Struggle to Survive Sexual Abuse as a Child*

"Karen Spears Zacharias's page-turner *The Murder Gene* shines on a number of levels. We know who executed these murders and assaults, but why? And what are the odds a young man would commit nearly identical gruesome, unpredictable crimes as that of his grandfather? Is there something in DNA that could forewarn us? Written with compassion and insight, *The Murder Gene* comes off as a cross between *Forensic Files* and *In Cold Blood.* I love this book."

—George Singleton, author of *You Want More: Selected Stories*

"*The Murder Gene* is a thorough report that looks into the genesis of the killer's acts. Seasoned author Karen Spears Zacharias takes the reader on a journey that includes not only the compelling story of the victims and the crimes against them, but she also scientifically dives into whether the murderer could have been predisposed to kill."

—Cathy Scott, *Los Angeles Times* bestselling author of *The Killing of Tupac Shakur*

"*The Murder Gene* is proof, yet again, that Zacharias has a strong passion for the truth. Her in-depth research, along with her humanity for the victims she is writing about, make this book a compulsive read."

—Angela Pursel, The Next Chapter Bookstore, Hermiston, Oregon

"Award-winning author Karen Spears Zacharias has done it again with *The Murder Gene*. Using her expertise as a former investigative journalist and her writer's gift of prose, Zacharias effortlessly weaves the science behind DNA with the intrigue of true crime. The result is a page turning by nature or nurture? *The Murder Gene* is bound to create robust discussions and will stay with the reader long after the last page has been read."

—Michael Morris, author of *Man in the Blue Moon*

The Murder Gene: A True Story

by Karen Spears Zacharias

© Copyright 2022 Karen Spears Zacharias

ISBN 978-1-64663-648-8

Book cover photography by Susie Stuvland

Published by

 köehlerbooks™

3705 Shore Drive
Virginia Beach, VA 23455
800-435-4811
www.koehlerbooks.com

THE
MURDER
GENE

A TRUE STORY

KAREN SPEARS ZACHARIAS

VIRGINIA BEACH
CAPE CHARLES

PREVIOUS WORKS

Christian Bend (Mercer University Press)

Burdy (Mercer)

Mother of Rain (Mercer)

A Silence of Mockingbirds (MacAdam/Cage Publishing)

Will Jesus Buy Me a Doublewide? 'Cause I Need More Room for My Plasma TV (Zondervan)

Where's Your Jesus Now? Examining How Fear Erodes Our Faith (Zondervan)

After the Flag Has Been Folded (William Morrow)

Benched: The Memoirs of Judge Rufe McCombs (Mercer)

TABLE OF CONTENTS

PART THREE: THE INHERITANCE

Some of us who seem quite nice people may, in fact, have made so little use of a good heredity and a good upbringing that we are really worse than those whom we regard as fiends.

—C.S. LEWIS

For George Venn who first believed

&

with great appreciation to all in pursuit of Science & Truth,

&

with great love to the grands whom I pray inherit only the good DNA

PROLOGUE

When I think about how he stalked her, watching her move from room to room at the Travelodge, stripping beds and picking up damp towels, it is easy for me to regard Luke Chang as a cold-blooded killer.

Who knows how long he'd stood on the steps outside Pendleton City Hall watching the dancer's body move about with grace and intention? Amyjane Brandhagen had only worked at the Oregon motel for a few days. Had Luke noticed the cheerful auburn-haired sprite on her first day of work? Or was that Tuesday, August 14, 2012, the very first time he'd seen her?

Had Amy, as homicide detectives later suggested, caught Luke's attention because she reminded him of Desiree, the wife he'd left behind in California when he went AWOL from the Marines a month prior? Could Desiree have been the one true love of Luke's life? Desiree claims theirs was a loveless contract marriage, initiated out of compassion on Luke's end and desperation on hers.

Luke doesn't like to talk about Desiree. He won't confirm or deny Desiree's side of the story that the two never had sex, never shared so much more than one kiss. Luke doesn't want to talk at all about

Desiree, or Amyjane, or his best friend Casey, or the family who had loved him so well the entire time he was growing up back in Morganton, North Carolina.

I wrote to him at the Oregon State Penitentiary in Salem, where he is serving out his sentence for the 2012 murder of Amyjane Brandhagen, and requested an interview. Luke declined my request. Whatever he had to say about the violence he's wrought in his life, Luke said in his post-arrest interviews. We will get to that later.

Luke (Lukah) Chang is the son of missionaries. His parents, Jay (Ge) and Heidi, bring the good news of Jesus Christ to all those they consider lost. For a season during his high school years, Luke also served on the mission field alongside his parents and younger sister Leah. A picture of the missionary family hangs on the wall at New Manna Baptist Church in Marion, North Carolina.

The county seat, Marion is a rural historic community located about halfway between Morganton and Asheville. Void of the box stores on the outskirts of most suburbs and given its isolated locale, some might even consider it a holler. Comprised of mostly working-class white families, Marion is the hometown of the enigmatic stage actress and director Barbara Loden and former North Carolina Tar Heels Coach Roy Williams. Loden left Marion at age fifteen, seeking fame and finding it in New York City after she became the mistress, and then wife, of Elia Kazan. Loden made it known that the reason she left Marion was to find the glamorous life that she lacked in North Carolina.[1]

Study the photo the Chang family sent out to help raise financial support for their work overseas, and it is Luke who appears to be the happiest. Leah, sitting next to him, is trying to smile without showing her teeth. Standing behind Luke, their mother Heidi is an imposing woman. Her shoulders and neck are tautly pulled back and her hips are thrust forward. She is clearly standing at attention like a good soldier in the Lord's Army. She looms over her husband, who is shorter by a couple of inches. Jay, his hands clasped behind his back, has a friendly, engaging smile. Luke favors his dad. Leah does as well.

The Chang family photo is just one of dozens and dozens of other missionary photos displayed outside the church's main sanctuary. New Manna is what some around these parts of North Carolina refer to as "that mega-church." It's difficult to determine where all the people come from given that Marion's population is barely over seven thousand and there's about a dozen churches in town, but the sizable parking lot is packed by the time Sunday morning service rolls around.

New Manna bills itself as "Old Fashioned. Independent. Fundamental. KJV." That last part—KJV—is code for Believers. It means that the only Bible they use is the King James Version. It also means that they take it literally, as in the Earth was created in six days and men are meant to rule over every creature, including women. This is a church where men are referred to as Brother and women as Sister. Men wear off-the-rack suits with wide-knotted ties. The women are all clothed in dresses, below the knee. There's no cleavage, no bare arms, no flesh exposed beyond their feet and face. A woman wearing slacks will be warmly welcomed, but little girls will stare and whisper questions to their mother about why that woman is not wearing a dress like them.

The people at New Manna still consider Luke "family." They are a closed-mouth group for whom loyalty has become a cult-like persuasion. They remain the home base church for Jay and Heidi's mission work, so there's a deep sense of protection for them. (So deep is that protection that emails sent to former youth members who no longer even live in North Carolina were quickly relayed back to staff members at the church warning them that a writer was snooping around asking questions about Luke.)

That clan behavior has also been applied to the church's founding pastor who was alleged to have "sexual indiscretions." That's code used by church authorities to hide either illicit affairs or sexual assaults. Catholics aren't the only faith group to provide cover for church leaders' wrongdoings. Fundamentalists do it, too. It wasn't until I showed up at the church and began speaking to people face-to-face that I finally was able to get Luke's former youth pastor to speak on the record.

Of all the troubling twists and turns of this story, I think that meeting with Brother Jason Garner and his wife, Sister Trisha, solidified the thing that I still find unsettling about the murder of Amyjane Brandhagen: this feeling that had Luke and Amyjane met as kids in a youth group, they would have made the best of friends. They had so much in common. While Amy wasn't the daughter of missionaries, her parents, Dave and Cathy Brandhagen, have long been widely respected as people of faith throughout the Pendleton, Oregon, community. The year she was murdered, Amy went on a mission trip to India, with Youth With A Mission (YWAM). She returned home with a bigger vision for herself and for the world. Amyjane's heart was wide open with love and hope for humanity. Sharing the love of Jesus with others was her daily mission. She had that in common with Luke's entire family.[2]

Luke and Amyjane were highly intellectual young people who loved to read and go on adventures. They were imaginative, creative souls. Both were regarded as good-hearted people, always eager to be a help to somebody in need. They were playful older siblings to their younger sisters. Amy was more gregarious than Luke, so she had a wider circle of friendships, but both found their strongest social interactions within the church. And both had mothers who they regarded as overprotective and overwrought at times. Mothers who wanted one thing most of all: to keep their children safe from the evils of the world.

When I think of Amy and Luke, I prefer to think of them as the friends they might have been, most assuredly would have been, had they met somewhere other than in room 233 on that fateful summer's day. Amy blissfully unaware of the evil that was waiting for her just beyond the bathroom door.

Murder had been on Luke's mind for some time. As he told detectives when he was finally arrested, he was deliberately waiting for the exact right moment, the right victim. Just as his grandfather before him had done.

CHAPTER ONE

There is no sign now of the Rabbit Lady along North Carolina Highway 64, south of Morganton, North Carolina. She has been a long time gone now, says the man who lives in the one-story ranch house he bought some years ago from the Rabbit Lady and her husband. The current homeowner, Shane Jarvis, walked me around the property where Heidi and Jay raised Luke and Leah. Pointing to a thicket of towering bamboo in a field back beyond the house, Shane complained, "I have chopped that bamboo all the way down to the dirt and it still comes back."[1]

Bamboo is a fertile mother; some shoots can grow four feet in twenty-four hours. Known as the poor man's timber, bamboo belongs in the grass family. Cut the greening stalks down to the bare earth the way the homeowner along North Carolina's US Route 64 did and it will grow right back up as if to spite a person. That's because underneath that vertical stalk growing skyward, a horizontal stem known as a rhizome forms the veins of new growth.

As sturdy as it is stubborn, bamboo has been lauded throughout history for its versatility. The poet Shui noted, "Bamboo shoot for food, bamboo tile for house making, bamboo hat for rain sheltering, bamboo wood for fuel, bamboo skin for clothing, bamboo paper for writing and bamboo shoes for foot wearing, that is the life, we cannot do without bamboo."[2]

"I wonder why the Chang family planted it?" I asked.

"I think they planted it for food," Shane replied.

Leah Chang never mentioned eating bamboo in any of the many conversations she and I had about her growing up in North Carolina. Now a resident of Arizona, Leah remembers her growing up years with a mixture of romanticism and fatalism. While she never mentioned going hungry, she often spoke of the poverty that earned her mother Heidi the title of "Rabbit Lady" around rural Burke County.

"For a long time after I bought the place, people would stop here looking to buy rabbits. One old colored woman told me that the Chang family would sell the rabbits for $8 apiece, skinned. I guess that was a pretty good deal," Shane said.

The Changs were desperate to sell their home in 2009 when Shane Jarvis bought it. "They were preparing to go on a mission trip overseas," he recalled. Luke and Leah were in their teens. Heidi's father, Gene Dale Lincoln, had passed away in May of 2006, thereby relieving her of the familial ties that had kept her tied down in North Carolina.

Jay and Heidi Chang's family first came to North Carolina when their babies were toddling. Jay accepted a call to pastor at the community's Hmong Church, but for reasons nobody is willing to speak about, that call had not lasted long. Jay left that ministry and went to work in one of Morganton's furniture manufacturers. It was low-paying work (not that ministering to a growing community of Hmong people was lucrative by any means), but money was never Jay's primary pursuit. Taking God's message of love and forgiveness to a wounded world was the thing that motivated him.

To a person unaccustomed to the ways of fervently religious people in the foothills of Appalachia, Jay and Heidi might appear unsophisticated. But my own people are from nearby Sullivan and Hawkins County, Tennessee. Reading over Heidi and Jay's mission statement, I hear the echoes of people I have known all my live-long days: "Team up with other like-faith missionaries, to work with our people. Win Souls. Discipleship. Train Leaders."[3] In other words, carry out the Great Commission: go unto the ends of the earth and make disciples of all people. This notion of winning souls to Christ was common talk among my people, and among most of the people raised up in the mountain hollers of Appalachia.

On November 12, 2009, Jay and Heidi Chang signed the deed to their one-acre property over to Shane Jarvis. The rabbit pen where Jay and Luke skinned rabbits and Heidi sold them to locals for $8 each is still standing, but it is hidden from view by the bamboo that has continued to propagate like rabbits turned loose.

Regeneration. In theology the term means to be reborn, to be made new again. The belief that Jesus Christ died for our sins, and through his sacrifice we are made whole again. This is the belief system that Jay and Heidi Chang continue to embrace and that they worked to instill in their children and even now are continuing to share with the Hmong and other tribal people of Northern Thailand. It is a belief system that Leah has embraced, and for a time so did Luke. Perhaps he still does.

But regeneration isn't solely a belief system: it is also a biological function. Cut a jellyfish in half and it can grow back the half you cut off. Slice off a salamander's leg and it will grow back. Researchers at Harvard University have recently been able to identify the DNA on-and-off switches that seems to make whole-body regeneration possible. "What we found is that this one master gene comes and activates genes that are turning on during regeneration," stated researcher Andrew Gehrke.[4]

That "master gene" Gehrke referred to is known as the early growth response gene, or EGR. The EGR controls a web of genomes much like the master switch that controls all the hundreds of lights on a Christmas tree. Without the main switch, the tree stays dark, but if the switch is working, the entire tree lights up. It's the same with the EGR. When it is working properly, it lights up thousands of genomes, making it possible for a salamander to regrow a leg, for a jellyfish to replicate its missing half.

Up until recently, researchers were not able to identify why whole-body regeneration works in some species, as with certain worms, and only in a limited way with others, such as with humans, but the discovery of this master switch suggests this ability has a lot to do with the wiring of the DNA.

"There are many species that can regenerate, and others that can't," explained Mansi Srivastava, assistant professor of Organismic and Evolutionary Biology at Harvard. "But it turns out if you compare genomes across all animals, most of the genes that we have are also found in the three-banded panther worm, so we think that some of these answers are probably not going to come from whether or not certain genes are present, but from how they are wired or networked together."

Figuring out how someone is wired is what has brought me to North Carolina. This was not my first trip to Morganton. I've been coming back to the area since Luke Chang was arrested and convicted for the 2012 murder of Amyjane Brandhagen of Pendleton, Oregon. Luke did not know Amyjane. I did.

It's easy to imagine the reasons why somebody might kill somebody they know—jealousy, power, greed, unbridled rage. It's a lot more troubling trying to figure out why a person goes about killing somebody they don't know at all. Shane Jarvis did not know Luke was in prison until I stood in his yard with him that March afternoon and told him that young Luke Chang had murdered a girl I once knew.

Shane didn't know the Chang children. His dealings with Jay and Heidi were brief and all business. The only thing he really knew about the former owners was that they appeared to be good Christian people. There was nothing to suggest to Shane, or anyone else, that here among the shadows of blue pastoral hills, a murderer was emerging. As we walked over a carpet of clover, he told me that old timers around these hills refer to the region as "Bloody Burke County."

The name has several references, depending upon which old timer you ask. Some tell stories of the car wrecks suffered by those willing to run moonshine up and down the roadways. But for Shane, the name Bloody Burke County came from the story of fifteen-year-old Gladys Kincaid. The young teen was reportedly walking home from work at the local hosiery mill when she was assaulted and bludgeoned to death in June 1927.

The suspected killer, Broadus Miller, was working a construction job near where Gladys was last seen. Miller, a black man, was a convicted felon who had served time in South Carolina for the alleged murder of a black woman. At the trial for that first murder, a court-appointed psychiatrist testified that Miller suffered from severe mental illness. After the death of Kincaid, a two-week manhunt ensued. Burke County's attorney and would-be senator, Sam Evin, Jr., had Miller declared an "outlaw," which under North Carolina law meant anyone could shoot to kill Miller.[5]

For two weeks, a posse tracked him before one of their members stumbled into him in a town about thirty miles away from Morganton. A trigger-happy posse member shot and killed him. The posse then brought his body back to the courthouse in Morganton and put it on display. Over six thousand people traipsed by the courthouse that afternoon to gawk at the dead black man who they insisted had murdered the young white girl. Miller was never given a trial, not that it would have been a fair one anyway.

Decades prior to Miller's murder, Morganton was the site of yet another gruesome killing. In December 1831, a few days prior to Christmas, Johnny Silver was reportedly hacked to death and dismembered in a cabin he shared with his wife, Frankie, and their year-old daughter. Frankie was arrested and convicted for chopping up her husband. She was eighteen at the time. Without question, "Bloody Burke County" has a history deserving of its title.

Maybe counties possess their own sort of DNA, that of poverty, of greed, of lust and longings, of racism, and of fanaticism. There is so much to DNA and our connection to those who've come before us that we have yet to comprehend. Is it possible that some type of regeneration applies to those who murder, too?

The bamboo growing along Shane's property is decades old now. It knows nothing of the history of Bloody Burke County. The bamboo that covers the pen where Luke and his father once slaughtered rabbits has formed another outcropping along the neighbor's property line, creating a point of consternation for Shane Jarvis, who is quick to point out, "I didn't plant it there. It just grew up on its own."

Some murders can seem as random as an outcropping of bamboo. A girl can be making beds in a hotel room humming a praise tune, counting down the number of rooms she has left to clean before clocking out for the day, completely unaware that death is lurking just beyond the bathroom door. Or perhaps she's pitching a tent in a rural campground one afternoon, thinking about the friends she is supposed to meet up with the next day, completely unaware that she will be dead by daybreak.

Is it possible that some killers grow up with a flawed DNA code passed through a family line, skipping some generations, showing up in others, like an outcropping of bamboo that's jumped from the rabbit pen to the neighbor's fence line?

CHAPTER TWO

Hamley's Café is tucked into a quiet corner near the leather shop where the renowned Hamley's western saddles are hammered out. I grabbed a coffee and joined Pendleton Police Chief Stuart Roberts at one of the small bistro tables. Chief Roberts has the bearing of a West Point Cadet. He is firm of build, square-jawed, and possesses steel-rod posture. He looks directly at people when he speaks to them, whether that's over a cup of coffee or before a roomful of fraught citizens. He's faced his share of such citizens during his long career, which is why we were meeting.[1]

The August prior, Amyjane Brandhagen, a beloved girl throughout the community, was found murdered at a local hotel where she worked. Months passed and no arrests had been made. I knew Roberts from my former work as a cop reporter and because he assisted me on a previous book about child abuse. As the search for Amyjane's murderer went on, I sent Chief Roberts an email and asked if he thought there might be a story in this. We were meeting to talk about the case.

Under his leadership, Pendleton Police had worked the case for months and were no closer to solving it than they had been on that August afternoon in 2012, when Amyjane's fully clothed body was discovered in a pool of blood on a bathroom floor. But those particular details of the murder were not yet known. For nearly a year, the community-at-large did not know the manner of Amyjane's death, and on that morning, neither did I. Roberts is circumspect and professional. He kept the details of Amy's murder under wraps.

"It might have been someone who stopped in town for a while, then left," Chief Roberts began. "Somebody just passing through. Somebody searching for another victim."

"A serial killer?" I asked.

"Possibly."

CHAPTER THREE

E ver since the late 1800s, when Sir Archibald Garrod took to studying the underlying cause of black urine disease (alkaptonuria), researchers from a broad spectrum of scientific fields have pondered and explored DNA and its expressions in our daily lives.[1] Garrod, a physician at St. Bartholomew's Hospital in London, figured out that the rare black urine was not the result of some bacterial infection as was previously believed but rather the result of a genetic defect more common among those who had offspring with close kin. The defect Garrod isolated was a missing enzyme that aided in the chemical breakdown of protein. Garrod referred to these recessive traits as "inborn errors." Given that black urine disease is common among the offspring of first cousins, Garrod may very well have called these genetic chemical mutations as "inbred errors."[2]

Black urine was the first disease to be identified as the result of a gene mutation. Its discovery fueled the search for the sequencing that is the Human Genome, allowing for Chinese scientist He Jiankui to create the world's first gene-edited babies. The possibility of editing a human gene probably never crossed the mind of Sir Garrod, but when it comes to DNA, all discovery is interlocked. Just as the double helix of the DNA is both repetitive and adaptive, so is the research, which builds on that which came before.

Garrod's work would not have been possible had it not been for the work of Gregor Mendel, the monk who in the mid-1800s first documented recessive and dominant traits while crossbreeding pea plants.[3] Moreover, it is doubtful that Francis Crick and James Watson would have discovered the double helix of DNA had it not been for the singularly focused work of Rosalind Franklin; for it was the young chemist's research data and her X-ray photograph, used without her consent, that gave Watson and Crick the information they lacked.[4] A utilization for which they then gained worldwide accolades and fame. These two men not only failed to credit Franklin but engaged in deriding her, which speaks volumes about misogyny and the ongoing competitiveness of DNA research. There is not only fame to be had but wealth to be gained. And not just wealth, but power, for the ability to edit a human's DNA is not just stuff for the fiction marketplace. It is driven by investors in markets worldwide.

We assume that people have a basic knowledge of DNA, the way we assume they have a basic understanding of the Constitution of the United States, but as recent politics have proven, such knowledge is often highly distorted. There is a lot of misinformation or missing information. What exactly is DNA? Every person emerges from their mother's womb carrying their very own internal programming code. Our codes are embedded in a molecule with the very wonky name of deoxyribonucleic acid, or DNA, a much more manageable moniker. Each person's code is replicated from their biological parents, passed down from one generation to the next, like a treasured letter of historical significance. A person's genome is simply the sum of one's hereditary information.

The question of whether a murder gene can be passed along is the same sort of question that led a Dutch woman to University Hospital in the Netherlands. She was seeking help with the men in her family, all of whom had a propensity toward violent behavior. One tried to rape a sister. Another tried to run his boss over with a car. Another forced a sister to undress at knifepoint. The woman wondered if there was something hereditary that caused her brothers and her son to act out in such deviant ways.[5]

At that time—1978—genetic researchers did not have the means to determine whether there was an aggressive gene or not. But today, thanks in part to geneticist Han Brunner and his team at that Netherlands hospital, it is a well-established fact that a genetic defect on the X chromosome can be an indicator for violent behavior.[6] Collecting data from twenty-eight members of the Dutch family over the course of several years, Brunner and his team finally identified a marker for violence on the X chromosome. The violent men in the Dutch family all possessed this marker.

That marker is what is commonly referred to today as the MAOA gene, more properly known as the enzyme Monoamine oxidase A. The enzyme's purpose is to break down chemicals that trigger, or inhibit, nerve impulses. Those three chemicals include norepinephrine, which raises blood pressure and increases alertness, and serotonin and dopamine, which regulate a person's mood and alertness. Imbalances in any of these mood-altering chemicals are commonly found in people with psychiatric problems.

Brunner and his team reasoned that if the MAOA gene was not functioning properly, in other words, not producing enough of the enzyme, then an excess of the neurotransmitters, dopamine, serotonin, and norepinephrine would accumulate in the men's systems and likely be present in their urine. When the Netherland researchers tested the urine of the men, they found excess levels of all three chemicals. It is the excess level of these neurotransmitters that can predispose men to violence when they are under stress. Researchers noted that two of the Dutch men had committed arson following the death of a loved one. Who knew a person's pee could hold such a chilling secret?

We all carry the MAOA gene. It is the mutation or flaws in the gene that create the problem. Advances in DNA research have allowed geneticists to further identify even more specific markers.

They know, for instance, that it is the 2R variant of the MAOA that has the strongest genetic propensity for violence. Without getting into the tall weeds, the 2R variant refers to two repeat sequences within the DNA. Some refer to this as the "extreme warrior gene."[7]

"Warrior gene" may seem like a much more honorable label than "murder gene," but the biological impact upon males with the 2R variant is the same—antisocial behaviors and a propensity toward violence. Some refer to the MAOA-2R as the much more inflammatory "psycho gene."

This defect is carried on the X chromosome from mothers to sons. Women have two X chromosomes, so if they have the marker on one chromosome, the other chromosome will usually cancel it out. That makes women carriers for the violence gene but not commonly susceptible to the aggression flaw themselves.

Does this mean that if your son has the MAOA-2R gene that he's going to grow up and become a serial killer? No, not at all. Researchers have found that having the MAOA-2R does not by itself make a person violent. There are many complex factors that compel a small subset of the male population to commit murder or some other violent activity. Not every murderer has the gene variant identified by Brunner, nor does there seem to be a single gene mutation that compels aggression.

While it is true that Brunner's study and additional twins' studies have noted a correlation of impulsive violence that suggests a heritability factor of 44 to 72 percent, this behavioral trait isn't the result of a single gene or a single gene mutation, said Dr. Jan Vevera. Vevera is professor at the Psychiatric Clinic, Charles University Prague, where he also teaches medical ethics and continues research on the root causes of violence.[8]

In our 2020 email exchange, Dr. Vevera explained that one study he conducted involved an analysis of 281 males from four separate Czech prisons. These men, who had completed a structured psychiatric assessment, were diagnosed with extreme impulse for violence. The men then provided blood samples for genetic analysis. Their DNA was genotyped, and any rare copy mutations were identified. Of the 281 males, 264 participants were revealed to have rare mutations in 754 genes, with some of those mutations repeating more than once, some as many as twenty-five times. Many of those impacted genes were associated with X-linked disorders affecting adult behaviors, cognition, learning, intelligence, and neurodevelopment. The Czech study confirmed that 123 of the 281 participants (44 percent) had at least one mutation that was directly or indirectly relevant to impulsive violence. In other words, there isn't just one single gene that can be inherited that will make a man prone to extreme violence, but rather a cluster of mutations that can be passed along. As Dr. Vevera explained, "Impulsively violent behavior is a complex trait that results from multiple genetic and environmental factors, but the specific genes and their variants (mutations) conferring risk are poorly characterized and largely unknown."

It is because of the complexity of mutation that the risk for heritability remains the subject of ongoing research. Science is not yet able to identify who among us might be a violent threat. "With the hope of a better understanding by analyzing extreme cases and their individual genetic profiles, looking specifically at any rare variants that would be significant for biological knowledge and for potential clinical treatment," he added.

But it is with that research for heritability for violence in mind that we must take a closer look at the stories of Gene Dale Lincoln and his grandson Luke Chang. What prompted these two men to kill women with whom they had no prior relationship four decades apart from one another? Is it possible, even probable, that grandfather and grandson shared a code for murder?

PART ONE:

THE GRANDFATHER GENE

CHAPTER FOUR

Nancy Laws pulled into Michigan's King Lake campground late Saturday afternoon. There were only a half dozen or so spots at the lake's north end. Fishermen came and went throughout the day seeking to hook a perch or northern pike, but most returned home by nightfall.[1]

Nancy chose a wide-open spot next to the only other camper in sight. She figured if she set her tent just right, she'd have a front-flap view of the lake in time for sunset. She sat idling the car, the radio cranked up. The O'Jays were playing "Love Train." The beat fit Nancy's mood. Sometimes a girl needs to go off by herself, soak her bare feet in river mud, and think of nothing other than the next stanza of a good tune. Turning off the ignition, Nancy exited the car and continued to hum the song as she opened the trunk. She lugged out her gear, placing it on a nearby picnic table.

"Hey, can I give you hand with that?"

Nancy jumped. Dropping the box of food back into the trunk, she turned quickly around to face a stranger.

"I'm sorry," the man said. "I didn't mean to startle you." He was standing only a couple of feet from her. Too close for comfort.

"I didn't hear you walking up," Nancy replied. She gave a jittery laugh and flicked her thick dark bangs away from her eyes, squinting against the sun.

"Gene Dale Lincoln," the fellow said as he stuck out his hand and smiled. "That's my tent." He nodded his head toward the other camp site, about one hundred yards away.

Nancy shook her head in recognition. "Saw it when I drove up." She carried the box of food stuff to the table and set it down.

"Can I give you some help?" Gene offered again.

Nancy paused for a moment, studying the situation. It was already past four o'clock. She could use some help getting her tent up before dark. She noticed the ring on the man's wedding finger. Maybe his wife was around nearby. Maybe she was in the tent taking a nap or reading a book.

Gene, a lean man, wasn't particularly threatening-looking. The dark stubble on his face was a sign he hadn't used a razor in a week or so. He wore jeans and a dark T-shirt with a logo she couldn't quite make out. His fingernails were grimy, the way you'd expect a fisherman's to be. He had a boyish grin, friendly. His eyes scrunched up at the corners. *Smiling eyes, like the song*, Nancy thought. Gene looked to be only a few years older than her, early thirties maybe.

"Thanks, I could use some help," she said.

Gene took a final drag from his cigarette and flipped the butt toward the lake. A bird trilled from a tree nearby. A raft of ducks rose up from the water and took to the sky. Gene and Nancy glanced toward the lake at the sound of wings cutting through the air. The waters of the five hundred–acre lake lapped a low riff.

The two chatted courteously as they set up her tent. Gene told Nancy he'd just gotten up there the day before. He said that other than fishermen coming and going throughout the day, it was a relatively peaceful place. "A good place for escaping," he said. Nancy never asked what it was he was trying to get away from. Prying into other people's business wasn't her way.

"Got some beer over at my camp. You are welcome to come on over."

"Thanks," Nancy replied. She studied his wedding finger for a second. Gene shoved his hands into his jean pockets. Maybe his wife wasn't nearby. Maybe the two of them were out in the darkening woods alone. "I'm pretty bushed. Been a long day."

"Yeah, I hear you," Gene said.

"I'll probably fix something to eat, then turn in for the night."

"Gotta rustle me something up to eat myself."

"Oh," Nancy said. "I thought perhaps your wife might be doing that."

Gene smashed a pinecone under the tip of his boot, reached into his shirt pocket and tapped out another cigarette, then offered the pack to Nancy.

"No thanks," she said. "Never got into the habit."

"Good for you," Gene said. "Bad habits are my best friends." He took a drag, expelling smoke out the other side of his mouth in one long stream. "I do have a wife, but she's not with me."

Nancy didn't need to know why this stranger's wife wasn't with him. She appreciated his help, but right now she wanted him to go off and leave her alone. There was something about him that made her feel small and threatened. Maybe it was the way he kept eyeing her breasts. The married men Nancy knew might notice her breasts in passing, but they never indulged anything more than that. Gene was obvious about his fixation with her boobs. Nancy wished she was wearing her college sweatshirt instead of the tight-fitting tee.

If Gene's wife had been with him, she might have invited the two of them to join her for supper, but she wasn't about to ask him to stick around. Now that the sun had set, the lavender gloaming meant that she needed to get a fire built before pitch-black arrived. She started breaking twigs and piling them in the fire pit. She had no reply to Gene's comment about his wife not being with him.

"Thanks again for your help," she said.

"No problem." He knew he was making her uncomfortable. As he began moseying off toward his own camp, Gene said, "Give a holler if you need anything else."

Nancy nodded and waved. She hoped it would be daylight before she saw Gene Lincoln again.

Back at camp, Gene stacked some thin branches into his own fire pit and blew on the red embers of a dying fire until it reignited. He added a couple of logs that had been left behind by whomever camped there before him. Gene watched the dancing shadows cast by the fire. Finishing off another beer, he kept thinking about Nancy. He could hear her singing some song he didn't recognize. She could carry a tune better than most gals he'd heard in the juke joints he frequented.

"A pretty young girl like her has no business up here in the woods all by herself," Gene said as he poked the fire with a longer branch. "No telling what might happen to her."

CHAPTER FIVE

Nobody leaves home expecting to be murdered by nightfall. Across this country, people rise up at first light of day, pour themselves a cup of coffee, turn on the radio, hop in a steamy shower, and run through a list of all they have to accomplish without it once entering their minds that sometime during the day they will encounter a murderer.

Certainly, nothing could have been further from the mind of Nancy Ellen Laws as she prepared for that camping trip in June of 1973. Wisconsin was enjoying a fortunate streak of warm weather. Temperatures were in the seventies, perfect camping weather considering the heat and mosquitoes soon to come.

Nancy was ready for a break from her studies at the University of Wisconsin-Milwaukee. She envied her older sister Judy, who was married and had a family of her own. Sometimes Nancy wished she was married and living someplace besides her parents' home. One day soon, maybe, she'd get a big job in the city like their older brother Bill. Nancy couldn't wait to get out on her own. She was tired of the constant bickering between her and her young brother. Three years her junior, Richard, twenty-one, was prone to treat Nancy as if he was the boss of her.

The last time she was over at her sister's, Nancy confided to Judy that she was looking forward to going off by herself for a while.

"I'm camping with some friends. You and Fred will have to call Mom if you need a sitter." Nancy traced droplets on the iced tea glass Judy handed her.

"When?" Judy asked.

"Right after school's out." Nancy sipped the tea.

"Who are you camping with?" Removing a pot of boiling pasta from the stove, Judy drained it over the sink, pulling her face back from the steam puff.

"Just some friends from school," Nancy said.

"You should leave an itinerary of your plans with Mom. Just in case somebody needs to get ahold of you." Judy dumped the pasta in the rooster-adorned bowl that had been a wedding gift from somebody. She couldn't remember who.

"You are such a worry-wart," Nancy chided.

"I'm a mother," Judy replied. "It's part of my job."

"Yeah, well you aren't MY mother. You and Richard both are bossier than Mom."

"If you didn't play up your position as Miss Independent, maybe we wouldn't be so inclined to boss you."

"Oh, pleeaseee," Nancy said, rolling her eyes at her big sis.

It was the last time the two of them would ever speak.

A week later, Nancy swung her sleeping bag into the trunk of her Chevy Nova parked in the driveway of her parents' Waukesha home. Strangers who considered her 5'3" petite frame might think Nancy too dainty of a girl to be an experienced camper. They would have been sorely mistaken. Anything her brothers could do, Nancy could do better. There was the fire of an explorer in her emerald eyes.

Humming John Denver's "Rocky Mountain High," Nancy headed back into the house for her foot locker. She'd packed it the night before with her clothes, folding in several pairs of shorts, a couple of pair of jeans, a swimsuit, long-sleeve shirts, and a jacket for the cooler nights. She'd also tossed in her sketchpad and charcoal pencils. Nancy planned to check out some of the ghost towns along Michigan's Upper Peninsula. She hoped to capture some of those haunted buildings. If her sketches turned out, she might even transform them into paintings later. She'd split her food items between a separate smaller box and a cooler. She double-checked the Nova's trunk, making sure she had packed her sleeping bag.

Nancy was the Laws family's free spirit. She'd grown up in Waukesha, a bedroom community to Milwaukee. The town was once known for its healing hot springs, but those had long since dried up. Nancy was well-loved throughout the community. Her artistic abilities and her love of singing made her a much sought-after local talent. It helped that Nancy was willing to volunteer for just about anything anybody needed. Every stranger was simply a friend yet unknown to Nancy.

Gene Dale Lincoln would be the last stranger Nancy would ever meet, and he was no friend. By the time he turned thirty-seven, Gene thought life might be much easier than it was during that time when he was dishonorably discharged from the Army. Gene never spoke about the wrongdoings that led to his departing ways with the military. He figured that was nobody's business but his. Besides, hadn't he made good on his life? For a little while, anyway?

He'd managed to earn his associates degree in arts from Ferris State College in Big Rapids, Michigan, and had gone to work for the city's public works crew. Gene managed to parlay his experience into a better-paying job as the city tax assessor in Ironwood, Michigan, and later as the Alger County tax director. He liked working with the city, liked the power it gave him over others and the respect it demanded from them. He even relished the jokes made about him being the tax collector. He knew that embedded in those jokes was a hint of fear. Gene wanted people to fear him, a little at first, then a lot.

Gene and Doris Hill married in 1968 and had four kids in quick succession without much thought of what kind of stress that might thrust upon them. In 1973, Gene left his tax job, not happily or willfully, and found work in a factory. Gene didn't like to talk about why he was no longer working for the city. The loss ate at him. It was demeaning to go from a comfortable position of power to a job most any willing laborer could do. It diminishes a person in any untold number of ways to lose a job with rank, no matter the whys. But Gene knew it was even more demeaning when the reason for being fired was a fella's own damn fault.

The job loss had put additional strain on his marriage. Doris was even less happy than he was about the job change, if that was possible. Despite his best efforts, there were always more bills than money. Gene didn't like to admit it, but the Army wasn't the only place he had trouble holding down a job. His drinking had led to all that job instability, but Gene Lincoln wasn't about to own up to that, either. Owning up to stuff wasn't his way.

Sometime around Memorial Day (he couldn't remember if it was before the holiday or after it), he and Doris had another brawl. Ticked off, Gene left. He couldn't remember whose idea it was that he just "get the hell out." It didn't really matter, did it? He packed up his 1963 Rambler with his clothes, a tent, and a sleeping bag, and left. Just up and left it all behind. Doris. The kids. His job. The fighting. All of it.

He drove to Newberry, thinking he'd camp somewhere out by Tahquamenon Falls, where the water runs rusty on account of the cedar swamps, the land of Longfellow's *Hiawatha*:

> *I am weary of your quarrels,*
> *Weary of your wars and bloodshed,*
> *Weary of your prayers for vengeance,*
> *Of your wranglings and dissensions.*
> *All your strength is in your union,*
> *All your danger is in discord...*

Gene's sole intention as he drove was to put a lot of distance between him and the missus. He knew people in Munising, but he was in no mood to stop and visit. He blew right past the highway exits, past the truck stops and package stores. He'd already filled the car at one of those quick-stop marts, where he also picked up a six-pack of beer. He'd gone through half of it before he reached Newberry.

He camped there for a few days, keeping to himself mostly. Gene would much rather watch people than interact with them. He liked sitting on a log around the campfire, smoking and drinking. Being in the woods gave Gene the opportunity to consider all the ways in which his life had gone off the rails. The jobs gained and lost. The friends. Now the wife and kids. He pondered their fight over and over in his head, growing angrier with Doris at each replay. They fought over everything. They fought over nothing. It was always that way with the two of them. Sober people might get over such frays, but thanks to alcohol, other people's ordinary squabbles turned into raucous melees in the Lincoln household.

After a few days in the woods, a better man might have turned his car south toward home. A better man might have sought out his wife, begged her forgiveness, and promised to get help with his drinking. He might have urged her to get help with her drinking, too. Marriages don't start out in a burst of anger. Why do so many bust up that way? A better man might have told his wife that they both needed counseling. But Gene Dale Lincoln was not a better man. Poor choices had hounded him all his life, and turning that Rambler on the highway toward King Lake would prove to be his most deadly decision yet.

CHAPTER SIX

Doni Heuss considered herself to be a most fortunate girl growing up as she was in one of the smattering of houses circling Michigan's Hungerford Lake. The thirty-five-acre lake is surrounded by acres of limey woods and miles of mossy trails. People from throughout the region spend summers at the lake, but she and her thirteen siblings got to live there year-round. For a twelve-year-old girl who loved the outdoors, the lakeside community was a magical place to grow up. Almost like a fairytale, replete with the bitchy stepmom and a dangerous villain.[1]

Doni's mother had fought for custody of her five children during an embittered divorce from Doni's father, but their mother had no secure means of support, so the court awarded the couple's kids to John Heuss. Soon afterward, Doni's father remarried. Doni's stepmom was a devout Catholic woman who had nine children of her own. The family required two vehicles to drive to Mass every Sunday. The new Mrs. Heuss was devout in all the rigid ways. Rosaries were employed as a tool of discipline rather than a meditative means for drawing nearer to the heart of God. As one of the eldest, Doni was often required to look after her younger siblings. Too often, Mrs. Heuss treated Doni more like an indentured servant than a daughter.

Doni suspected her stepmom resented her. She seemed to nurture a jealousy toward her. Perhaps understandable given that birthing nine kids takes a toll on a woman's body. Muscles once taut are stretched into loose putty. It was probably difficult to find the time to wash her own face, much less get dolled up. At age twelve, Doni was one of the tallest in her class and already more woman than girl. The lush dark hair grazing her lean waist was the envy of other girls, and Doni's tanned legs were a constant source of distraction for boys.

John Heuss began most mornings with a walk around the lake with his daughter, another slight that irked his new wife. Doni didn't care. She ignored her stepmom's snide comments. The young girl enjoyed the early morning time alone with her dad. They didn't talk much, if at all, but were content to greet the newness of each day in the presence of one another. More tomboy than girly-girl, Doni shrugged off any slights, perceived or real, and relished their father-daughter ritual.

John Heuss bred the love of the outdoors into Doni. The two enjoyed the pine straw crunching underfoot as they watched the morning mist rise in a Holy Ghost cloud over the lake. It was on those morning walkabouts that Doni learned a person doesn't have to say anything to commune with another. Doni knew her father needed the quiet as much as she did, given the everyday ruckus of the household.

It was the daily commotion Doni sought to avoid on Monday, July 23, 1973, as she and her best friend Pam made plans to camp. Doni hightailed it to the lake with friends as often as she could during the summer months—to swim, to boat, to fish, to sunbathe, to camp, or to ride horses on one of the many fern-embossed trails.

Pam and Doni didn't attend the same school. Life at the lake had brought the two together and made them besties. Pam, thirteen, didn't tell her parents she and Doni were camping that night because she knew her parents would forbid it. Instead, she told her folks she was spending the night with Doni. It wasn't a lie exactly, but it wasn't the whole truth, either.

The girls had befriended a college student who had a campsite near Hungerford Road, not far from the Heuss home. There was a pathway behind Doni's house that led straight to the lake. The girls asked their college friend if they could sleep in his tent that night. "Sure," he said. "I'm headed out for a couple of days. Help yourself to any of my gear. You can help keep an eye on the place while I'm gone."

Since camp was already set up, the girls didn't have to do anything except enjoy themselves. They spent the day at the lake, swimming and sunbathing.

"I have to be back home in the morning. to babysit or else I'll be in big trouble," Doni said, handing a towel to Pam.

"I know. Me too," Pam said. She patted her legs, then draped the towel over her shoulders. "Mom told me to be home early."

"I managed to sneak out some marshmallows," Doni said. Treats were rare around the Heuss household; getting them out of the house without being stopped by the food police was rarer yet.

"Far out! We can roast them later."

"It's colder out here than it was in the water," Doni said. She stretched out on her belly across the beach towel. A breeze pushed soft waves to shore.

"Here," Pam said. She handed Doni a red T-shirt.

Doni sat up and pulled on the shirt. "You hungry yet?"

"I could eat," Pam replied. "You done swimming?"

"Yeah," Doni said. She pulled shorts on over her bathing suit bottom and began picking up their floats and towels. Pam grabbed the transistor radio and slipped on her flip-flops. "Some of the guys said they might drop by later. Jerry said he might take us for a ride if we want."

After the girls changed out of their wet bathing suits and slipped into dry clothing, they made themselves bologna sandwiches and sat around the wooden spool that served as the camp table.

"Looks like somebody is over there," Doni said. She nodded in the direction of the campsite kitty-corner from theirs. The campsite itself was hidden by brush. A person would need to turn up a lane and go back into thicker woods to reach it, but Doni could see someone or something rustling around in that direction.

"You think they could help us light this lantern?" Pam asked. The sun was setting behind a straggle of trees. "I can't seem to figure out how to make this thing work." She fiddled with it some more before shoving the last bite of bologna into her mouth. "C'mon, let's go be neighborly," she ordered.

"You got the lantern?" Doni asked.

"Yep."

Gene Lincoln was sitting outside his tent drinking a beer. He'd lost count of how many he'd drank that day. Not that he cared. He saw the two girls turn the corner and walk up the dirt path. He had no idea what they were doing. One was carrying what looked to be a camp lantern. They were headed straight toward his camp.

"Good afternoon, ladies," he said as the two girls approached. He took another swig of beer, swishing it over his tongue like a daily mouthwash before swallowing.

"Hey," Pam said. "We're your neighbors." She pointed through the trees.

Gene looked over his shoulder in the direction she was pointing. "Mmm. I drove by that place yesterday. You got that tent pitched pretty close to the road."

"Oh, it's not ours," Pam replied. "It's a friend's tent. He's letting us borrow it for the night." She held up the lantern. "This is his, too, but I can't figure out how to turn it on."

Gene took the lantern, turned it over, pulled the batteries out, reinserted them. Slipped them out again, fished his pocketknife out of his jean pocket, tinkered with the connection, then put the batteries back in and turned the lantern on. "There you go." He handed the lantern back. "It's working now. Not sure how much life is left in the batteries, though. Might run out before the night is up."

"Thanks," Pam said.

"No problem," Gene replied. "Can I get you girls a beer?"

Both Doni and Pam shook their heads and giggled. They'd never had an adult offer them a beer before. They didn't know if he was teasing or not, but they didn't dare take one from him. That was probably illegal or something. He was old enough to be their dad. Or at least he looked it, even though he wasn't nearly as clean cut as either of their dads. Bristly stubble crusted his face. His dark hair was ill-kept, greasy, like he hadn't shampooed it in a month of Sundays. A foul stench shrouded him. The girls kept an easy breathing distance from him.

"You sure?" Gene held the can out, then took another long swallow from it.

"We're sure," Doni said. "We've got to be getting back."

"Thanks again for your help," Pam said, holding up the lantern. She'd turned it off to save the battery life.

"Suit yourself," Gene said. "But if you get thirsty, come on back."

The girls hurried off to their own camp.

"He was kind of creepy," Pam said as soon as she was far enough away that he couldn't hear her.

"Yeah," Doni agreed. "And he smelled like stinky butt."

"How do you know what stinky butt smells like?" Pam asked, laughing.

"I've changed enough diapers, that's how!"

Shortly around eight thirty that evening, friends dropped by their camp. Jerry, Doug, and Kenny were hangout friends, nothing more. The boys and girls had all grown up together, like cousins. They'd spent most of their childhood summers messing around at the lake.

That night they roasted those marshmallows Doni had snuck out of the house. The five of them gathered around the campfire talking about school and which sports teams they'd try out for the coming school year and which teachers they hoped they'd never get in high school. They were there underneath those towering silent trees, laughing and swapping stories when Gene drove up and rolled down the window.

"Hey, I'm headed to town," Gene called out. "Can I pick up anything for you?" He was really headed to the little country market to get some more beer. In truth, he was eager to buy some alcohol for the underage kids, especially the pretty girls with the long, tanned legs.

"Do you know him?" Jerry whispered.

"Yeah, we met him earlier today," Pam said.

"Who is he?"

"I dunno. Some guy camping out over yonder," Doni said, nodding toward the nearby site. "He needs a bath." The boys all laughed.

"He helped us light our lantern when we couldn't get it to work," Pam added.

Jerry raised up the Coke can he was sipping from, pointed it toward the blue car. "Thanks anyway, buddy. We're all good here."

"Suit yourself," Gene said. He gave a slight wave and then drove off, leaving a puff of dust drifting toward the teens.

The group quickly turned back to the fire and their conversations, giving no further thought to the smelly man. Later, Doni and Pam piled into Jerry's car and rode into town with their friends. Had either girls' parents known, they would have been placed on restriction for the rest of the summer. Their sneaking off that way would complicate matters for the girls in ways they could not yet foresee.

By the time Gene returned to the lake, the teens were long gone. Their camp was dark. No fire. No lights. No laughter. Gene popped open one of the beers and sat at his camp, thinking on those girls and their long, tanned legs. He was still sitting by the red ember fire drinking beer when Jerry and the others dropped Doni and Pam back at their camp, shortly after midnight. Gene was already halfway through another six-pack.

In the hush of early morning, moments before the sun popped up flamingo pink over the misty lake, Pam woke with a start. "Did you hear that?" she whispered, shoving Doni's shoulder.

"Yeah," Doni said, sitting up. She rubbed her eyes, ran her hand through her hair, swiping it back off her face. The two girls waited turtle-still, their ears attuned to the outside. Somewhere across the lake, a dog barked. Woodland birds trilled their morning songs. Then it came—a scratching just beyond the tent flap. Rabbit? No. Bigger than that. Deer? They wouldn't get that close to humans, which they could smell. A bear? Perhaps. That frightened them.

"What was that?" Doni asked, her eyes darting around the tent. A bear could be upon them before either of them knew it.

Pam shrugged. "I don't know, but that's not the sound that woke me."

"Yeah, me neither," Doni responded. "It was much louder than that."

The girls sat up out of their sleeping bags and put on their tennis shoes. They'd slept in their shorts and T-shirts, so they were already dressed for the day.

"It sounded like a car door slamming. Maybe John's back from his trip already?" Pam said. Perhaps the college friend who had loaned them his campsite had come back early for some reason.

"I doubt it," Doni said. There was a rustling sound outside the tent again. "Did you hear that?"

"Yeah," Pam replied. Just then, the alarm Pam set the night before went off, startling both girls. Grabbing the clock, Pam punched the "OFF" button, while Doni began unzipping the tent flap.

"I'm gonna go check it out," she said.

"Me too," Pam replied, right on Doni's heels.

Gene leapt out from the shadowy side of the tent where he'd been waiting. He grabbed Doni from behind, flashed the shiny blade of a butcher knife, and pressed it up against her throat. "Don't you dare scream, bitch!"

Doni screamed anyway. Pam jumped out of the tent, unsure of what Doni was hollering about. Gene pushed the terrified Doni up against the campsite's wooden spool, then to his car, which he had parked nearby. It was his car that had first woken the girls only minutes earlier.

This very same car in which Gene had stuffed Nancy Laws's dead body only weeks earlier. He pressed the knife hard at Doni's throat.

Pam saw the fear on Doni's face and that long butcher knife against her girlfriend's throat, and she took off running. She could hear Doni's screams as she ran: "LET ME GO! LET ME GO! WHAT ARE YOU DOING?" Gene was too busy struggling with Doni to give Pam chase.

Pam ran and ran. She did not look back.

Doni was fighting with all her might, but the twelve-year-old was no match for a grown man. Amped by the thrill of killing, Gene yanked opened the car door and shoved Doni in. Terrified, she instinctively grabbed for the knife in his right hand and tried to jerk it away.

"YOU LITTLE BITCH!" Gene yelled, gripping the knife tighter, jerking it back, and slicing open Doni's hand as he did so. "MOVE!" He shoved her over to the passenger side door and crawled in behind the steering wheel. "TRY THAT AGAIN AND I WILL KILL YOU!"

Gene cranked the engine and pushed the gas pedal. He tried to keep control of the car with his left hand and Doni with the other. Doni reached for the doorknob. Her mind was racing, her heart pounding. She knew she had to make an escape or this man would surely do as he threatened and kill her. If she could get the door open, she would make a run for it. Doni was certain she could outrun him.

She worked quickly, sliding her hand up and down the door in search of a handle to grab. She kept her eyes on Gene the whole time as he struggled with wheel and the knife. His eyes darted about, the look of an animal cornered. He was sweating profusely, and every time he cursed at her, spit flew from his lips. A Bible verse she had heard came to mind: "And Jesus asked him his name and he replied 'Legion' for many demons had entered him." She grabbed more furiously for the door handle but could not find it. She looked away from Gene, at the door. That's when she saw it.

There was no door handle, only a small knob where the handle should have been. Doni thought she might puke with fear. Gene had removed the handles in anticipation of his young prey's efforts to escape. Now she was the animal cornered. Anger rose up from a place deep within her. She had to escape. The window was rolled up.

She wasn't strong enough to break it, but she slapped her open palm at it anyway, leaving a streak of blood from the knife's cuts.

"STOP IT, BITCH!" Gene yelled as he pushed the silver blade up against her throat again.

Pam ran west, past the lane where the girls had met Gene the night before. She ran down the moss-covered trail to a camper trailer. Pounding on the door with both fists, she screamed, "HELP ME! HELP! HE'S GOT DONI! HE'S GOT HER!"

Gary Routley and his wife Bobbie Jo heard the pounding and the urgent cries of a young girl. Gary made it to the trailer's door in two leaps. Grabbing the sobbing teen, he yanked her into the trailer, quickly slamming the door behind him, unsure of what was threatening her.

"What's going on?" he asked, out of breath himself.

"HE'S GOT DONI!" Pam screamed. "HE'S GONNA KILL HER. YOU'VE GOT TO GO GET HER! HURRY! HE'LL KILL HER!"

The Routleys knew the young girls. The lake community was close-knit. All the locals knew one another, knew one another's kids, and watched out for each other. The couple had seen the girls earlier the evening prior. Gary got enough information from Pam to know that the man who took Doni had a knife. "You stay here with her," Gary instructed his wife. Pam was hysterical, clearly in shock. Pulling on his boots and grabbing his gun, Gary ran off in the direction of the girls' camp.

Gene looked over and smirked at Doni. "You're mine now, you little bitch!"

Doni replied with a kick to his right kidney. Gene clenched the knife between his teeth, grabbed hold of her foot, and held onto it. Doni jerked until she managed to pull her foot back and curled it up underneath her. She was crying, sobbing, terrified out of her mind.

"SHUT THE FUCK UP!" he ordered.

Between the crying and the stench of Gene, Doni could barely catch her breath. He was rank. The bottom of the camp toilet couldn't smell worse than Gene Dale Lincoln did at that moment. He was dressed in stained jeans and a yellowed T-shirt, which he'd covered with a flannel shirt so nasty there was no telling what color it had been new. He looked like one of the hitchhikers that her daddy would sometimes pass on excursions into town.

Gasping for air and desperate to escape, Doni reached for the crank of the passenger window and began rolling it down. He had not thought to remove the window crank. Reaching across the seat with his right hand, Gene slapped at her, but Doni was quicker.

"YOU FUCKING BITCH! I'M GONNA KILL YOU!" Gene yelled.

With the window down, Doni lunged for the steering wheel and jerked it to the right with all her body weight. The car swerved. The front tire struck a stump, causing Gene to yank the wheel wildly in the other direction. The car seized to a stop on an embankment. It stalled momentarily, giving Doni the one chance she'd prayed for.

The twelve-year-old flung herself out the passenger window, stumbled near the front tire, then rising, she took off running for dear life, oblivious to the blood streaming down her arm, onto her legs, the road. Doni had just one thought: RUN!

"FUCK!" Gene yelled. "FUCK!" He pitched the knife across the front seat where he'd held Doni captive and pounded the steering wheel with both hands. "Fucking bitch!" He knew better than to give chase. Throwing the car into reverse, he floored it. The cops would soon be after him. He had no time to waste chasing after a girl gone.

Doni ran straight for the Routleys', her instinct the same as Pam's: *Find an adult. Tell them what happened.* The girls had acted without thought on the mantra generations of parents and teachers had taught. *When in danger, find an adult you can trust.*

They both trusted the Routleys. Doni had no idea Gary was enroute to find her. They practically collided into each other on the path. Doni's hands were covered in blood. Hugging the sobbing girl, Gary guided Doni back to the trailer, bandaging her up as best he could until he and Bobbi Jo could get the bleeding and terrified girl to the hospital in Big Rapids.

Pam was still crying when the Routleys dropped her off at her home, explaining very briefly to her mother what little they knew: A man had tried to abduct Doni. Pam had made a run for it. Doni had escaped, but she was cut up badly. They were taking Doni to the hospital in town. Please call the police. And Doni's dad. Could they call him, too?

CHAPTER SEVEN

After the failed abduction of young Doni Heuss, Gene Lincoln went roaring out of the campgrounds at Hungerford Lake. He didn't get far. Big Rapids is about a twenty-minute drive away from the lake.

It was a familiar town to Gene. He had spent the last week of June and first week of July with Bill Olson, a friend and former coworker who lived in Big Rapids. At that time, Olson had no idea that Gene was a murderer. He only knew Gene and Doris had a bad row. It happened to a lot of married couples. Olson offered Gene a place to bunk for as long as he needed, but Olson was concerned. He could tell something was amiss with his pal.

Gene wasn't himself. He was disheveled for one. Dirty hair. Dirty clothes. Foul-smelling. He said he'd left Doris and the kids weeks ago after a particularly bad fight, and he made it clear he had no intentions of going back. Olson told Gene he was welcome to stay, but he was relieved when, after the Fourth of July, Gene left. He had spent most of that time with Olson in a stupor, drinking more than usual. His mind seemed to be elsewhere, not so much rattled as distracted.

When Gene left, he didn't take anything with him. Not even a trunk he'd hauled in from the car. Olson thought that was odd. Didn't he need the stuff in it? For weeks, the footlocker sat in the bedroom where Gene had left it. It wasn't until later, when the nightly news began reporting on an attempted kidnapping at Hungerford Lake, that Olson became suspicious and decided to open it up, see if there was anything of importance in it, since Gene had told Olson he might go camping up at Hungerford. What Olson found inside that trunk convinced him that his friend was far more disturbed than he ever imagined.[1]

The next day, Bill Olson called the police. He told them that his buddy Gene Lincoln may have had something to do with that kidnapping at Hungerford, and possibly that girl from over in Wisconsin, too, the one everybody was searching for. Olson had heard about the young woman from Waukesha who had gone missing. Newspapers and television stations throughout the region had reported on Nancy's mysterious disappearance. Her picture was often front and center in the newspaper.

The town's local paper, the *Waukesha Daily Freeman*, reported that Detective Robert Goetzelman, who was working the case, received a call on Tuesday, July 31st, from Olson. Olson said his buddy Gene had abruptly disappeared from his place in early July, but he had left behind a footlocker. Olson said that he had opened the trunk and discovered several female items in it—a woman's shirts, shorts, underwear, bras, a sketch pad with some sketches in it, some books, and shoes. Stuff that clearly didn't belong to the father of four.

"Any ID of any kind?" the detective asked.

"No," Bill Olson replied. "Nothing." He added that his friend Gene had been acting weird prior to taking off.

When he made the call, Olson didn't know that state police already had Gene Lincoln in their custody. They'd picked him up on Sunday, July 29th, hitchhiking off South Straits Highway and Michigan 68, a busy crossroads not far from the Sturgeon River. Gene didn't give the officers any information about who he was or what he was doing out that way. They arrested him for hitchhiking, but what police didn't say at the time was Gene fit the description of the man the young girl out at Hungerford Lake claimed had tried to kidnap her.

For the next three days, Gene Lincoln sat in jail knowing the wrongs he had done but convinced that the police didn't know. While they might be able to connect him to the abduction of the young girl at Hungerford Lake, Gene knew that without the body of Nancy Laws, there was no way police would be able to ever connect him to her.

What he hadn't counted on was being ratted out by a friend like Bill Olson. He went off and left all of Nancy Laws's belongings behind, never imagining that even if Olson rummaged through the trunk, he'd pick up the phone and call police.

However, armed with new information, a detective on the case called Nancy's parents. Reluctant to get their hopes up too much, he didn't mention everything Olson had told him. Instead, he asked if they had a list of items Nancy might have taken with her on that camping trip.

"I bought her a new pair of tennis shoes for the trip," Mrs. Laws replied.

"Can you describe them?" the detective asked.

"They were plain white tennis shoes. We bought them at the Boston Store at Bayshore Mall," Mrs. Laws replied.

The *Waukesha Daily Freeman* newspaper reported that inside the footlocker left at Olson's place was "an unusually shaped jar of chest rub." What that newspaper didn't report on at the time was an empty shoebox marked with a Boston Store logo. That box was the strongest lead yet that police had connecting Gene Lincoln to the still-missing Nancy Laws. Oh, and there was one other thing; Olson said that Gene had showed up at his place driving a blue Chevy Nova with Wisconsin license plate.

The missing gal's missing car.

CHAPTER EIGHT

fter the phone call with Olson, police renewed their efforts to find Nancy Laws and her missing car. Meanwhile, Gene Lincoln was being held at the Newaygo County Jail, charged with the suspected abduction of Doni Heuss.

On Thursday, August 2, 1973, just two days after Olson's call to local police, law enforcement conducted a helicopter search in Michigan's Upper Peninsula. Newaygo County Prosecutor Douglas Springstead took part in the search for the missing Wisconsin coed Nancy Laws.

The thirty-one-year-old Springstead was the county prosecutor for five years when the case of the missing Wisconsin girl came across his desk. A lot of the early investigation into the case fell to him. "At that time, we didn't have any officers certified for that kind of investigation. Some of the state police were, but not many. So I had to do it myself," Springstead said.[1]

The kidnapping of Doni Heuss was being handled by the sheriff's department since it fell within his jurisdiction, but the phone call from Bill Olson had prompted Springstead to begin an investigation into the disappearance of Nancy Laws. He worked the case the way he worked every case, methodically: "You talk to the victim and get their version. Then you work your way through that. I began with the girl."

Springstead was impressed with the composure of Doni Heuss. "She was courageous," he said. "Had she not escaped, Lincoln would have killed her." He recalled how Lincoln had cut her as Doni fought him off. "She jumped out that car window and got blood on the car door."

Springstead's suspicions about Lincoln's involvement with the murder of Nancy Laws were growing. "Once you work your way through the victim's testimony, you have to put information out into the public and wait for any witnesses to step forward."

Springstead relied on the newspapers and television to get the information to the public. While waiting for that help, he and law enforcement from a variety of jurisdictions continued to search the Huron National Forest for any sign of the missing girl. "For two weeks, I rode my motorcycle around out there, searching."

Gene Lincoln was a tax assessor. He knew the land. He knew exactly where to dump a body so that it would never be found. Springstead was hopeful that all their searching might turn up some sign of Nancy, since the fellow they had in custody wasn't talking. When he did speak, Gene Lincoln denied knowing anything about the missing girl.

"Care to explain how it is that you had her things in your possession, then?" detectives pressed him.

"I dunno what you are talking about," Gene replied. Police hadn't found him in possession of anything belonging to Nancy. Gene thought he had made sure of that. They had nothing more to go on than their suspicions.

Police knew he was lying, however. Gene was unaware that Nancy's parents had driven to Michigan to meet with Springstead and to look at the recovered footlocker, which they identified as belonging to their daughter.

Springstead was doubly disappointed then when the helicopter search turned up nothing on that first day. Despite covering tons of campsites, and an area about sixty miles long and thirty miles wide, the search had failed to yield any sign of the University of Wisconsin journalism student.

Despite the lack of a body, Springstead had little doubt that the man sitting in the Newaygo County Jail knew exactly what happened to the Wisconsin coed. He spent the weekend going over what evidence he did have: testimony of Doni Heuss, who had been abducted by Gene Lincoln but fought her way to safety. Springstead was sure had she not been such a scrappy girl, Doni would have faced the same fate as Nancy Laws, and even though Springstead wasn't quite sure yet what that fate was, he knew it wasn't good. He didn't expect police to find Nancy alive, if they ever found her at all.

Local authorities renewed their search on Monday, August 6th, expanding it north beyond Newaygo County to neighboring Wexford County. They were determined to cover every mile of Huron-Manistee National Forest if need be. If Gene Lincoln had killed Nancy Laws as they suspected, there was probably no better place to hide a body than in the shadows of 540,000 acres of hardwoods and red pines. Springstead was along for the ride.

This time they got lucky. They located Nancy's abandoned Chevy Nova off a two-lane road in a heavily brushed area of Wexford County. Exactly where Gene Lincoln had left it. The University of Wisconsin decal on the rear window and dent in the rear fender along with descriptions provided by Doni Heuss assured law enforcement they had the right vehicle.

The discovery of the car was not good news for Nancy's family, however. It meant what they most feared—that their daughter was not coming home. The *Waukesha Daily* reported police confirmed that Nancy Laws was believed to be dead, and they fully expected to find her body in Michigan's Upper Peninsula. Finding the car only renewed their commitment to find the missing coed.[2]

Springstead was coordinating with the Wisconsin police, the Michigan State Police, and the Newaygo County Sheriff, but the discovery of Nancy's vehicle meant that now he also had to deal with the FBI.

"They thought they had jurisdiction because the car was found on federal property, but she wasn't killed there," Springstead explained.

All these decades later, the former prosecutor harbors an abiding resentment toward the FBI. "We had worked primarily with the Wisconsin police because that's where the girl lived," Springstead said. "They were going to go to her home to try and collect fingerprints and hair samples for the investigation, but before they got there, the FBI jumped the case and collected the stuff to send off to their labs. If they hadn't done that, I could have brought the samples to the lab in Lansing and had the results back the next day. The FBI stalled our investigation. I wasn't happy about that. I raised a particular hell with FBI over that. I thought their jumping the gun was a cheap trick."

Meanwhile, the suspect remained at the Newaygo County Jail, where he was undergoing mental tests to determine his ability to stand trial. His arraignment for the Doni Heuss kidnapping charge was set for Wednesday, August 22nd. Springstead filed the charges against Lincoln: "One Gene Dale Lincoln willfully, maliciously and without lawful authority did forcibly confine and imprison one Donata Heuss within this state against her will."[3]

Prior to the arraignment, John Shepherd was appointed by the court to represent Gene Lincoln, who claimed he could not afford an attorney of his own. Shepherd was born and raised in Newaygo County and had a long history with the local courts. His grandfather had served as the county clerk, and his father was a county surveyor. During World War II, Shepherd enlisted in the US Air Force and attended officer's training school at Yale. He was stationed in Guam throughout the war, where he rose to the rank of captain. Upon returning stateside, he earned his law degree, then began his career first as a White Cloud county commissioner before becoming an assistant county prosecutor.

The fact that he had been a prosecutor at one time gave Shepherd an edge another defense attorney might have lacked. "He knew how to make a deal with the prosecutor's office," Springstead said.

Judge Harold Van Domelen conducted Gene's arraignment on the Doni Heuss kidnapping case. Prior to being elected as a circuit court judge, Van Domelen spent over a decade as a prosecutor. The former Navy veteran had been a minesweeper during the invasion at Normandy, so he was well-equipped at reading situations. The first hearing was to the point. Van Domelen began by asking whether Gene Lincoln understood that the charges against him could carry a life sentence. Shepherd said yes, his client understood that and was ready to enter a plea.

Judge Van Domelen directed his questions to Gene.

"How old are you, Mr. Lincoln?"

"I'm thirty-seven, sir."

"Do you fully understand the nature of the charge?"

"Yes, sir, I believe so, sir."

"And you have discussed it completely with your attorney, Mr. Shepherd?"

"Yes, sir, I have, Your Honor."

"And do you understand that the maximum sentence involved in this is life or any term of years in prison?"

"Yes, sir, Your Honor."

"And you understand that the minimum sentence and the maximum sentence is in the discretion of the Court?"

"Yes, Your Honor."

"And do you understand that this Court has no idea what that sentence is going to be at this time?"

"I understand that, yes."

Judge Van Domelen then explained that prior to sentencing he would have to study any pre-sentencing reports sent to him and take those into consideration. He inquired whether the defendant was on a prior parole or probation at the time of the abduction. Gene assured the judge he was not.[4]

That was a fact that Springstead could never reconcile given the nature of the charges that Gene would face in the case of Nancy

Laws—he had no prior criminal history. Nothing. "There was nothing to indicate he would do the things he did," Springstead said. "He was unremarkable. Quiet. An average guy of average height, a little on the thin side. I thought it was really strange that he had no criminal history because he was a really sick puppy. I had never heard of necrophilia until Gene Lincoln came along." Necrophilia is the sexual attraction to a corpse, something Gene Lincoln engaged in.

The judge asked if Gene understood that entering a plea would waive all his constitutional rights to a trial, either before the court or a jury, and to do so would also mean that any assumption of innocence would be waived, as well as the right to have any previous confessions or admissions was made voluntarily.

"Have you discussed that with your attorney?"

"Yes, Your Honor."

"Now, you have the right to plead guilty; you have the right to plead not guilty; or you have the right to remain silent. Which do you choose to do?"

"I choose to plead guilty, Your Honor."

"Is your plea voluntary?"

"Yes, Your Honor. Entirely."

After clarifying that he had not been coerced or bribed in any fashion for his plea, Judge Van Domelen asked Gene about the specifics of the kidnapping charge.

"What happened on the 24th of July?"

"I pulled up in front of a tent in which she and another girl were sleeping. Guess this was very early morning and . . ."

"About what time would you say it was?"

"It was shortly after daylight, perhaps six o'clock somewhere."

"Well, six o'clock."

"I don't really know, Your Honor. The girls in question walked out of the tent. I grabbed her. I had a knife in one hand and grabbed her. I put her in the car and got in the car and started to drive off. I drove from one side of the road to the other, and I believe I got stuck, and she left the car and I drove off. I believe in the operation she was cut. I didn't realize this until later, but evidently she was cut."

"You said she came out of the tent. Did you ask her to come out?" the judge asked.

"She happened to be coming out of the tent," Gene replied.

"And you grabbed ahold of her?"

"Yes, I believe so."

"Did you have a weapon at that time?"

"Yes, I had a knife."

The courtroom was quiet. The breath of the guards grew shallow. The only sound other than the interaction between Gene and the judge was the clicking of the court recorder.

"And what type of knife was that? Was it a hunting knife?"

"No, it was a household knife."

"A butcher knife?"

"Yes, I guess you could call it that."

The judge asked Gene how long the blade was; he replied it was the average butcher knife. Gene denied that he placed the knife at Doni's throat, but he added the caveat that he, too, was "confused on what happened." It's a statement he repeated when he told the judge he couldn't remember if Doni was screaming or not. (She was.)

"Was it your intention to drive away with her?" the judge asked.

"Yes."

"Against her will?"

"Yeah, it must have been," Gene replied.

"In other words, you're pleading guilty to the charge of kidnapping?"

"Yes, Your Honor."

"Your plea of guilty is hereby accepted. You will be referred to the Probation Department for pre-sentence investigation, and you will be detained in the Newaygo County Jail awaiting sentence without bond."

With a slight bang of the gavel, Judge Van Domelen brought the arraignment to an end, and deputies led the shackled father away.

The former county tax assessor would have time to reflect again upon that argument he had with Doris and how his anger had become a wildfire, scorching everything in its path.

CHAPTER NINE

Police notified Nancy's parents of their daughter's murder on Thursday, September 6, 1973, one month to the day after Nancy's abandoned car had been found.[1]

What police didn't tell the Laws at the time was that Baraga County's Prosecuting Attorney Hubert Mather had cut Lincoln a sweet deal: *Help us recover Nancy's body and we will make sure you are only charged with manslaughter.* Mather made the deal without first consulting with Nancy's parents or Judge Van Domelen. Mather's actions would infuriate the judge and cause the Laws family immense grief. Nancy's father disagreed vehemently with Mather's plan, even if it meant recovering his daughter's body. "Evidently the charge was agreed upon before we were asked for any of our ideas or attitudes," Robert Laws told the *Waukesha Daily Freeman.* "We were not consulted."

Lincoln could have easily received a life sentence solely on the charge of kidnapping twelve-year-old Doni Heuss, but Mather insisted that Lincoln would never have served any time for the murder of Nancy Laws had he not promised Lincoln such a sweet deal. "There never would have been a case at all if the charge hadn't been reduced to manslaughter," Mather said.

But Mather's position defied what compelled Lincoln to confess to the murder in the first place—the discovery of Lincoln's own vehicle, a 1963 Rambler station wagon. The abandoned car was found in a remote area of the Grand Sable State Forest in Michigan's Upper Peninsula. Sheriff Harold Heikkinen of L'Anse notified the Waukesha police, who then notified Mather.

Appearing before Judge Harold Van Domelen in Newago County on Thursday, September 6th, the same day he confessed to the murder of Nancy Laws, Lincoln was sentenced for the abduction of Doni Heuss:

"Now, you're telling me that you took her against her will, put her in the car, and drove off with her against her will," Judge Van Domelen asked.

"That's correct, Your Honor."

"Is there anything else that you wish to say at this time?" the judge asked.

"Not at this time, Your Honor."

"All right. It is the judgment of the Court that you be committed to the Department of Corrections to serve not less than fifteen years and not more than twenty-five years in such penal institution as the Department of Corrections may select."

The day he was sentenced for kidnapping a twelve-year-old at Hungerford Lake, Lincoln gave lawmen a detailed map of the place where he had buried the missing twenty-four-year-old from Waukesha. The *Ironwood Daily Globe* reported, "Authorities found Miss Laws's partially decomposed body buried in about four feet of earth at the edge of the Grand Sable State Forest in Alger County, about twenty-five miles northeast of Munising."

The very city where this father of four had once held a very reputable job in the tax assessor's office. Since Lincoln had committed crimes in differing counties in Michigan, there were several courts involved, a couple of different judges, prosecutors, and defense attorneys—court appointed, of course, since Lincoln claimed to be too poor to afford one. Not to mention, numerous detectives and investigators and police officers from varying jurisdictions.

Lincoln confessed to the crimes in Waukesha, Wisconsin—Nancy Laws's hometown—but the murder happened in Baraga County, Michigan. The attempted abduction of Doni Heuss happened in Newaygo County, Michigan. Law enforcement officials in Michigan had a headache on their hands having to coordinate criminal investigations, subsequent criminal charges, and prosecutions. Lincoln was costing taxpayers in both states a substantial amount of money, not to mention grief of the worst sort.

On Thursday, the 8th day of November, the State of Michigan brought the case of manslaughter against Gene Dale Lincoln in Baraga County Circuit Court. The Honorable Stephen D. Condon, circuit judge, presided over the arraignment.

Judge Condon began by asking Lincoln why he was pleading guilty.

"Because I am guilty," Lincoln replied.

"Has your plea of guilty been induced by any promises of leniency from the prosecutor's office, the sheriff's office, or any other law enforcement?" Judge Condon asked.

"No," Lincoln replied.

Judge Condon, aware of the deal Mather had made, turned to the prosecutor. "It's my understanding that you entered into an agreement with the defendant or his former counsel with reference to the filing of the charges here."

"Yes," Mather replied.

"All right, I'd request you state it for the record."

Condon explained that despite three months of investigation and searching by Michigan and Wisconsin and federal authorities, no one had a clue of the whereabouts of the body of Nancy Laws.

"Without this knowledge, there was no basis for filing a charge, and her disappearance and any crime connected with it would remain unsolved," Mather said. "The only suspect, Gene Dale Lincoln, was about to be sentenced on a kidnapping conviction, and he might receive a long prison sentence, an event which would terminate this investigation."

Mather went on to say that he discussed the matter with John Shepherd, Lincoln's attorney in the kidnapping case, and they agreed to a reduced charge of manslaughter if Lincoln would tell authorities where to find Nancy's body.

"It was a decision on my part to accept the only proposal the defendant would make, namely, to lead officers to the location of Miss Laws's body in return for a commitment on my part to not prosecute him on a charge greater than manslaughter, which carries a maximum sentence of fifteen years. The investigating officers were in full agreement with this decision, and about eight hours after this agreement, Miss Laws's body was located over one hundred miles from where it is believed she died."

Judge Condon, along with many others, was clearly not happy with Mather's deal making. He became even more disturbed by it as he questioned Lincoln about the details of Nancy Laws's murder.

"Where did you meet Nancy Laws?" Judge Condon asked.

"I met her in the park," the defendant replied.

"When?"

"It was about a day and half before the incident."

"That would be the first or second of June?" the judge attempted to clarify.

"It was a Saturday. I believe that would be the second of June."

"How did the meeting take place?"

"She came into the park, and I helped her put up her tent."

Lincoln went on to say because it was a small campground, their tents were only about one hundred feet apart. There were only half a dozen or so camp spots in the very primitive and remote area. Lincoln said the two of them spoke at length that first night, outside their respective tents.

"Now the next day would be approximately the third of June?"

"Yes, it was a Sunday, Your Honor."

"What transpired then?" Judge Condon pursued this line of questioning to make a record of all the wrongs that Gene Lincoln committed and so that the victim's family could have some insight into what had happened to their daughter.

"Oh, we talked off and on during the day, and we talked until very late into the night."

"Any drinking?"

"On my part, yes."

"Did Miss Laws have any?"

"No."

"How much did you have?"

"I had a couple of six-packs," Gene Lincoln replied.

"Was there a relationship between you and Miss Laws up to this point?"

"No, Your Honor."

"Did you have a sexual relationship?"

"No, Your Honor."

"All right. Go ahead and explain to me what transpired this Sunday evening," Judge Condon ordered.

"It was extremely late, and the conversation turned to sexual matters, and an argument pursued. And I can't give you the exact wordage of the argument except it was related to sexual matters," Gene Lincoln recounted. "And the verbal argument led to the exchange of blows, and it ended up she grabbed a plastic flashlight, and I grabbed a wrench, which I had been working on her car with earlier in the evening, and I began hitting her. And I just kept hitting her. When I was done, she was dead."

"This argument that you had with reference to her on sexual matters, your intention was to have intercourse with her?" Judge Condon asked.

"Yes."

"Is there any particular reason that you can give me as to why you grabbed the wrench and assaulted her with it?"

"I can't come up with a real good reason for myself, Your Honor, and I don't think I can come up with a real good reason for you, either. I just reached a state of rage that I had never reached before. I had never been like that before." Gene Lincoln was attempting to dismiss his own culpability.

"Your rage was brought about as a result of Miss Laws's refusal to have sex with you?" Judge Condon was not about to let Gene Lincoln place any blame on his victim.

"I think it was far more than that, Your Honor. I think it goes back farther than that night, to my being separated from my family."

"Do you recall about what time this assault took place?"

"It was extremely late. It may have been as late at two o'clock in the evening," Lincoln said.

"What did you do after the assault?"

"I just sat for a while and my mind began to straighten out and I realized that I had to do something, morning was coming very shortly. So I drove my car and parked it in the area in the woods, and I gathered up all of her stuff and all of my stuff and her body and I loaded it all into her car. It probably took me several hours to do that. It wasn't too long after daylight that I left there because I realized that it was Monday morning and probably someone would be around just after daylight."

"And where did you place Miss Laws's body?" Judge Condon asked.

"I placed it in the trunk."

"Between the time you assaulted her and the time you placed her body in the trunk, did you carry on any sexual intercourse with this woman?"

"Yes," Gene Lincoln confirmed.

"Did you have intercourse with her on more than one occasion between the time that you assaulted her and the time you placed her in the trunk?" Judge Condon knew that Gene Lincoln had sexual relations with a dead body. He wanted Lincoln to be clear about it for the court record.

"I don't know," Gene Lincoln said, refusing this time to admit to such a blunt acknowledgement of his necrophilia.

"All right. What did you do then?" the judge asked.

"I left the campground and proceeded to the Marquette area. I bought some gasoline, and I realized I couldn't go driving around with a body in the trunk, so I purchased a shovel, and then I went to the area the body was found in Alger County. It was early afternoon by the time I reached there, and of course, I hadn't slept the night before, so I just pitched my tent in the campground and relaxed. The body was still in the trunk. I got up the next morning, and I placed the body where it was subsequently found."

"Approximately what time of day was it when you proceeded to bury this body?"

"It would have been Tuesday morning. It was probably between eight o'clock and ten o'clock in the morning."

"You left the King Lake area with the body in the trunk, and you did not dispose of the body until approximately twenty-four hours later, is that correct?" Judge Condon was showing how egregious it was for the prosecuting attorney to make a deal with Lincoln, letting him off on only a manslaughter charge when he clearly had tried to cover up the rape and murder of Nancy Laws.

"That's correct. By the time I reached the area, I was so tired I just collapsed and woke up the next morning, then disposed of the body."

"What clothing was on the body when you disposed of it?"

"There was no clothing on the body."

"Completely naked?"

"Yes."

"After the burial, what did you proceed to do then?"

"I went to Big Rapids. I knew some people there. I realized it was just a matter of time until I was arrested, so where I went wasn't too important."

"When were you arrested?"

"The 28th of July."

"And the purpose of your being arrested was what? What was the reason?"

"I was arrested on the charge down in Newago County."

"Kidnapping?"

"Yes."

Clearly, Judge Condon was infuriated over the deal Mather reached with Lincoln. Body or no body. It appeared to the judge that the murderer was playing the system. He ordered Lincoln back to jail while he considered the confession and the charge of manslaughter.

Judge Condon reconvened the court on Tuesday, November 13th. He did not come to court in an indulgent mood. "Upon careful review," he began, "the Court finds that the defendant's plea of guilty to the charge of manslaughter is not freely and voluntarily made. It is obvious to the Court that the defendant's plea of guilty was made and induced because of the prosecutor's bargain not to charge the defendant with a crime greater than manslaughter in return for the disclosure of the whereabouts of the dead body of Nancy Laws."[2]

Condon went on to note that the prior sentencing in Newago County for kidnapping made any sentence he would administer null and void. "Such a sentence would be an absolute nullity and of no effect or consequence." Additionally, Judge Condon said, the facts of the case did not support the charge of manslaughter. Thus, he ruled, Lincoln's guilty plea to manslaughter was invalid: "The defendant's plea of guilty is not accepted. It is rejected by the court. Accordingly, a guilty plea will not be entered. I can neither condone or approve of the plea-bargaining agreement. The decision and determination by the prosecuting attorney to file an information in this Court charging the defendant with manslaughter was not based on any factual background or findings of fact, but on the contrary."

Mather acted beyond the scope of his authority when he bargained with Lincoln, the judge ruled: "The Court is of the opinion that the prosecuting attorney does not possess the prerogative of bargaining away the rights of the people of this State." And with that,

Judge Condon remanded the matter back to District Court of Baraga County for further action, with the instructions that Mather charge Lincoln with the crime of murder for the death, rape, and burial of Nancy Laws.

Mather did not take kindly to Judge Condon's rebuke. A couple of weeks later, he was back in court, this time appearing before Judge William Konstenius. Mather had given Lincoln his word that he would not file first-degree murder charges against him if Lincoln agreed to tell them where he'd buried Nancy Laws. Mather was hopeful the new judge would be more lenient than Condon.

It was unlawful for a trial court to adopt a prosecutorial function against a defendant, Mather argued. He brought up another case of Judge Condon's in which he had refused a plea deal. That case was overturned by the Michigan Supreme Court. Mather threatened that he would take the matter before the Supreme Court if the lower court didn't uphold the deal he'd made with Lincoln.

Judge Konstenius postponed the matter until January 29, 1974, but when he called the session to order, he was quick about delivering his verdict: "The Court is of the opinion that this matter calls for a swift, quick, and speedy disposition. The Court is going to determine that the proffered plea of guilty is freely, voluntarily, and understandingly made and the same will be entered. It is the judgment and sentence of this court that the defendant will be confined to the Michigan Department of Corrections, the Upper Peninsula Branch of the State Prison at Marquette for a maximum term of fifteen years, which is set by statute and a minimum term of ten years."[3] [4]

The judge awarded Lincoln credit for the 145 days already served. The sentence would run concurrently with the charge of kidnapping from Newago County. Nancy Laws's family was enraged over the verdict. Speaking to a reporter with the *Waukesha Daily Freeman*, Nancy's sister said, "I don't think it's right. Lincoln manipulated the law and this man will be out on the street again to prey on little girls."

Doni Heuss has lived in fear of that possibility her whole life long. Gene Lincoln, the former tax assessor and father of four, had gone off half-cocked for reasons even he couldn't explain. He killed and then raped a young college girl who had fought him. He'd carried her bloodied body around in a car for a day before burying her in a shallow grave. Then a month later, he attempted to abduct an even younger girl and would have undoubtedly raped and killed her given half a chance. But he was no match for twelve-year-old Doni Heuss. She'd escaped his death grip on her and has been fighting the stench of Gene Dale Lincoln and the ghost of him ever since.

Nancy Laws's sister got it right: Gene Dale Lincoln had gotten away with murder. Ten years later, he was released from prison. He took a bus to North Carolina, where his daughter and her husband and two children lived. Jay and Heidi Chang welcomed Gene into their home and into the lives of their children, seemingly without any hesitation at all.

PART TWO:

THE GRANDSON LUKE

CHAPTER TEN

t's awful growing up the child of a murderer.[1] Heidi Lincoln was only four when her father went to prison. Her mother, Doris Hill Lincoln, turned to welfare to support the family and to the bottle to bury her sorrows. Whatever drinking problems Doris had prior to her husband's killing spree intensified afterward. Heidi would confide to others that her mother was a "terrible alcoholic." Heidi and her three siblings knew the kind of poverty that invoked shame in children long before any of them understood that none of what transpired was their fault.

In the aftermath of her father's arrest, it fell to Heidi and her older sister to care for their younger brothers. Mostly it fell upon Heidi because Doris relied upon her the most. Sometimes when Doris went out drinking, she would take Heidi along. It was Heidi's job to get them both home safely. Heidi helped make sure her brothers were fed and dressed and ready for school. She assumed the mother role that Doris abdicated. There were times when things were so dire the state stepped in and took the children into protective custody. Once, when the state failed to find acceptable foster placement, Heidi and her siblings were reportedly put into a juvenile detention center.

Had she been born into another household, one that nurtured learning and rewarded intellect, Heidi might have risen to the ranks of a corporate CEO or a high-ranking military official. Even as a young girl, she was organized and smart as a whip. As a teen, she made no companion with despair but rather promised herself that she would live a better life than either her father or her mother. She would make better choices. Her children, if she ever had any, would not be wards of the court. She would be a good mother. The best of mothers. She had, after all, plenty of experience mothering others.

Had she come of age in a different era, or even a more progressive environment, she might have sought out a job at the Pentagon or at West Point. As a high schooler, Heidi entertained thoughts about a career in the military. The opportunity to experience other cultures appealed to her. Certainly, anything that would help her escape the poverty of her youth was worth considering. But while the military was a career option that brought boys admiration of the community, it was frowned upon for young ladies. Patriotism wasn't the only thing that ran deep in the woods of Wisconsin—misogyny did, too.

Girls who achieved success were the ones who found a husband who could support them well, provide a nice home, in a gated community preferably, safe from the perils of crime and drugs. Heidi grew up in a time and place where mores and expectations for girls were changing but had not yet changed enough. Sure, women had deployed with the troops to Vietnam, but they went primarily as nurses and Donut Dollies, traditional roles for women. Besides, Vietnam had long been over by the time Heidi reached high school.

Jay Chang was an infant when his father was killed in Vietnam. One of the Hmong people from Laos, Jay's father was fighting alongside South Vietnamese soldiers when he was killed in action. The year was 1965. One of the biggest battles of the Vietnam War was waged that November in the Ia Drang Valley. Americans and their allies suffered heavy casualties. With her husband dead, Jay's mother was left with very little choice or hope for a future. She did what millions of war-torn families did—she fled the country with her son. They left Laos, crossing the Mekong into Thailand. A refugee camp there became home to the young Jay. It was all the home he knew as a small boy.

By the war's end, an estimated 250,000 Hmong sought refuge in America. Jay and his mother were among them. Sponsored by a kindly woman in Chicago through the Catholic church, the young widow and her son found much to be hopeful about in their new environs. Chicago was unlike any place they'd been before. The Hmong people are by and large an agrarian culture, fishers and farmers. Urban life can be intimidating for those raised up in the quiet hillside communities of Laos and Thailand. It helped that Chicago is bordered by water. A change in landscapes can leave a person feeling disoriented, but bodies of water often offer an inviting and familiar refuge.

Jay Chang took to America, quickly mastering its language, the way he had the languages of his youth: Hmong, Thai, Laotian. Like many immigrant families, Jay's mother relied upon her son to do the translating for her. She retained the language of her youth, only learning the bits of English she needed to get by.

Perhaps not surprisingly, it was a Hispanic man who came to have the greatest influence on Jay's life. Joseph Espisto was in Bible College in Chicago when the two first met. Espisto drove the church bus that ferried children and teens back and forth for church services. A child who has grown up without a dad present, for whatever reason, hungers for men of character to step into their lives. Jay was no different that way. He'd never known what it was like to have a father present. He could only imagine what he was missing. Espisto, who wasn't that much older than Jay, was the perfect mentor to the young boy. A nurturer with a deep and abiding faith, Espisto became that person to whom Jay could always turn.

Espisto introduced Jay to the faith in Jesus that Jay claims to this day. "Immediately after I came to know Christ, I felt a deep desire to serve him," Jay said. "I was able to lead my mother, my aunt, and several of my cousins to the Lord."[2] He did this by encouraging his loved ones to attend church with him, the way he'd been encouraged to attend by Espisto. A year following his conversion to Christianity, Jay was called to the ministry. It was a call that continues to direct his life path.

Heidi's faith journey began at a grocery store. A fellow who bagged her groceries took a shine to her. When he finally worked up the nerve to ask her out, she said yes. Their first date was to a tent revival meeting. The message she heard at that meeting took root in Heidi's life. She had been unmoored her whole life long, never able to count on anyone or anything besides herself, really. The hope offered to her through the Word of God was exactly what Heidi needed. While her relationship with the grocery clerk didn't last, the one she formed with Jesus has.

Not long after that tent revival meeting, Jay offered Heidi a ride home from church. The two became friends during those rides to and from church. Jay, the immigrant, and Heidi, the outsider, had more in common than it might appear to the casual onlooker. They made a study in contrasts: Jay was about a head shorter than Heidi. Not at all a conventional beauty, Heidi possessed an exotic appeal with her mass of dark hair, creamy skin, and an engaging smile. Jay found her charming, a bright girl who thought deeply about matters of faith and the condition of humankind. Jay knew before their first date that she was the girl for him. "I want you to know up front that I am taking you on a date because I want to marry you," Jay said. It's a story they've repeated over the years, to the delight of family and friends.

Jay and Heidi were pronounced husband and wife on June 10, 1989. Jay, twenty-four, was already mapping out a career in ministry, attending Hyles-Anderson Bible College. Founded in 1972, the school was an outgrowth of the ministry of First Baptist Church of Hammond, Indiana.[3]

First Baptist has the largest membership in the state and has been in the top twenty nationally.[4] It's a genuine mega-church. At the time the Changs joined, the Independent Fundamentalist Baptist Church was under the direction of Pastor Jack Hyles. Hyles, who grew up in Texas, had abandoned the Southern Baptist traditions of his youth and embraced an even more legalistic and independent way of interpreting the Bible, a means by which the only person he was accountable to was himself. Religion was his vehicle to monetary gain.[5]

Hyles was more dictator than pastor, more of a Mob Boss than a Gentle Shepherd. He wrote books dictating every aspect of a person's life—from the clothing they were permitted to wear, to the form of corporal punishment they should employ with their children, to the amount of money they should be giving to the church.

The more Jack Hyles demanded of his congregants, the bigger his audience grew. The church reportedly had as many as fifty thousand attendees. A significant portion of that came from the bus ministry that First Baptist operated. Hyles sent buses from Hammond into the poorest neighborhoods in Chicago to collect children and haul them into church. It was that very program that got Jay involved with Hyles, his ministry, and the college. Jay and Heidi were at First Baptist during the height of Hyles's ministry and during the earliest years of their marriage. Years later, Hyles would be embroiled in charges of improper sexual conduct, and the church would be hit with a lawsuit regarding repeated offenses of sex abuse relating to that same bus ministry. The church settled out of court.

In March 1990, just days shy of her own twentieth birthday, Heidi gave birth to Luke Pobzeb Chang. (Dr. Vang Pobzeb was one of the most respected leaders and academics among the Hmong population. He was successful in getting the United Nations to recognize the Hmong, and he worked to raise awareness about the genocide of the Hmong taking place in Laos.[6])

Luke was a chubby-cheeked infant with a head full of dark hair and a sweet smile. Jay and Heidi were overjoyed. Having a family of their own was a chance to redeem the brokenness of their respective childhoods. Jay was a good father, eternally patient and wholly devoted to Heidi and Luke. Eighteen months after Luke was born,

Heidi gave birth to a daughter, Leah, an almost mirror twin of Luke, with dark hair and a dimpled smile.

Life took on a routine of feedings and diaper changes, of Little Golden Books and Bible stories read and repeated, of singing songs sung by mothers the world over—"Jesus Loves Me" and "This Little Light of Mine." It was a happy time for the family, a time of contentment and yet great yearnings for their family, for their community, and Jay's hope for the Hmong people. Jay and Heidi took to heart the admonition of the Great Commission: *"Therefore go and make disciples of all nations, baptizing them in the name of the Father and of the Son and of the Holy Spirit, and teaching them to obey everything I have commanded you. And surely, I am with you always, to the very end of the age."*[7]

Jay and Heidi had no idea how much they would come to rely on that promise of God. They had no way of knowing what the future held for them or their children.

CHAPTER ELEVEN

From the outskirts, Morganton, North Carolina, seems like any other town in the foothills of Appalachia. Located within the shadows of Black Mountain and the Pisgah National Forest, Morganton serves as a pit stop for Interstate 40 travelers. Up past the gas stations and fast-food joints are churches. Lots of churches: Baptist, Lutheran, Methodist, Episcopal, Assembly, Pentecostal, Catholic. There's even a First Hmong Baptist Church.

Morganton, along with neighboring Catawba County, comprised the largest Hmong population in North Carolina and one of the top four Hmong populations in the nation. Only California, Wisconsin, and Michigan had higher Hmong refugee populations. Between 1987 and 1994, an estimated fifty thousand Hmong immigrated to America.[1] Most came from the mountainous regions of Laos, Vietnam, and Thailand, which ensured that they were well-suited for rural North Carolina.

In 1994, when First Hmong Baptist called Jay to come serve as their pastor, the family packed up their belongings and left Indiana. The couple happily established their young family on a rural piece of property about five miles from downtown Morganton. The dense woods around the brick ranch house became Luke and Leah's playground.

For reasons nobody, not the Changs nor the church elders, wants to talk about, the job with the First Hmong Baptist was short-lived. It's never easy adjusting to a new pastor, and first pastorships are always a challenge due to the demands on family life and the lack of privacy. Trying to strike that balance between being a shepherd and headmaster is hard to do. The younger a pastor is, the more likely they are to lean into the role of headmaster more than that of shepherd. Whatever the reason, after a brief two years, Jay and the church elders agreed to part ways.

The Chang family didn't leave Burke County despite the job loss. It's more difficult to pack up and move once kids are in school. Luke was in first grade. Leah was enrolled in kindergarten. They both were attending a private Christian school in Morganton. Jay and Heidi made the decision to stay. Jay found a job at Milliken's, a carpet and floor covering manufacturer.[2] Burke and Catawba County were flourishing with carpet and furniture businesses in those days. Factory jobs were plentiful, perhaps because the pay was abysmal, even by North Carolina standards.

Supporting the family on one income was a challenge. Heidi, always resourceful, found ways to supplement the household budget. She and the kids raised rabbits, chickens, and ducks to sell. Luke and Leah became an integral part of the Chang cottage industry. By the time Leah was in second grade and Luke was in third, Heidi pulled the kids out of the Christian school and began to homeschool them. That freed up time for the kids to tend to the menagerie of animals that also included two dogs.

"The house was on an acre of land," Leah said. "Two sides of the property were woods. We got up at six o'clock every morning. We'd clean our rooms, take care of our house chores and the animals. School started promptly at eight o'clock. Mom would hand us the lesson plans. If we rushed through our schoolwork, we could be done within a couple of hours, usually by ten. Then we'd go outside and play until lunch. Afterward we'd play outside again until Dad got home. We'd do more chores after dinner, watch an hour of TV, and go to bed."

Luke and Leah stuck to this routine throughout the bulk of their childhood. Without much contact with other children, their world was pretty small and isolated. Their play was limited to the acre plot they roamed day in and day out.

Sometimes Leah looks back on that time fondly, recalling an almost idyllic childhood. But there are times now that Leah considers the isolation of it all. Does such isolation make a child feel safer in the world or more afraid of the world? What is communicated when children are raised in an environment where the outside world is considered dangerous? Where that child's family is regarded as "true believers" and others are regarded with suspicious skepticism? Could it be that the childhood Leah once regarded as idyllic was the very thing that prompted the darkness that would follow?

CHAPTER TWELVE

Luke and Leah were so close in age that they were more fraternal twins than mere siblings. In the North Carolina woodland of their youth, they would play the "us" and "them" games common to children: Cowboys vs. Indians. Cops vs. Robbers. Good Guys vs. Bad Guys. Boy vs. Girl. Leah never had to worry about whose side Luke was on—he was her champion, her co-conspirator in the world of Kid vs. Parent. And she was his.

But as they aged, their partnership changed. Luke had always been more like Heidi, quiet, reserved, studious. Never prone to revealing his emotions much. Luke got to where he'd rather stay indoors and read a book than to go outside and play in the woods. This was confusing to Leah. Why would anyone rather stay indoors? How boring!

Leah was a self-confessed tomboy. Growing up in Luke's shadow, she considered herself equally as capable of doing anything Luke could do. She could run as fast, jump as high, shimmy up a tree as quickly. Frogs and praying mantises fascinated her, as did the constellations in the night sky. The world felt like a place to be explored. Leah, ever the adventurer, couldn't wait to grow up and be on her own, make her own decisions, become the person God intended for her to become.

Pleasing God and pleasing her daddy was Leah's early ambitions. By the time she was a teenager, Leah had abandoned the idea of pleasing her mother. "We didn't get along. We never did, really. Luke was her favorite. She was really smart, and he was smart like her. He was a bookworm like her. He loved to read and to learn. I was the one who had to learn by repetition," Leah said.

Leah felt like she got on her mother's one last good nerve every single day. "I was the one who was always getting into trouble. Luke never had to be told to do things. I was the one who was always getting rebuked."

Rebuked, as in told to *straighten up and fly right. Or else.*

"I got blamed for whatever he did. It was like he was the perfect child. He was the angel, and I was the demon."

This growing divide within the family threatened the order Heidi sought. It might be a common thing in all families, this choosing of sides. At first, it seemed a given, this split between mother and daughter and father and son. Don't all kids feel like it's them against the grown-up world? Parents on one side, kids on the other?

Luke grew into a loner, void of the close friendships Leah cultivated. Much like Heidi, Luke preferred solitude to the company of others. "Mom didn't really have girlfriends," Leah recalled. "She was never girly or feminine. She had a few friends over the years but not many."

Instead of being recognized as "the pastor's wife," Heidi became known about Burke County as "the Rabbit Lady." Initially, Heidi started raising the rabbits for meat, a quick and easy source of protein for family dinners. But the fecundity of the rabbits ensured they could feed far more than a family of four, so Heidi and the kids joined the American Rabbit Breeders Association. Eventually, Leah and Luke would have as many as one hundred rabbits to tend to.

The marketing plan was simply a hand-painted sign along the well-traveled road in front of the property, alerting passing motorists of "Rabbits for sale." With each rabbit sold, Heidi would pass along a pamphlet on basic rabbit care, and tucked inside the pamphlet was a quick guide to the Plan of Salvation. Even in commerce, Heidi fulfilled the call of the Great Commission, ensuring that everyone should hear the Word of God.

Luke tended to the rabbits daily, alongside Leah, even though he had little interest in them other than the cash they provided. Luke was much more enthused about the fighting roosters his daddy bred. By 2003, there were nearly four thousand fighting cock operations in North Carolina. In 2005, Governor Mike Easley signed a bill declaring cockfighting a felony.[1] But for the most part, during the years Luke lived in Burke County, local officials looked the other way. There were far more serious crimes to worry about.

Did this father-son activity encourage Luke to normalize violence and develop a hunger for cruelty? Jay had grown up a young boy watching the bloody fights that ensued when two angry roosters were tossed together; it is often a fight to the death. Neither Jay nor Heidi appeared to have any reservations about letting Luke be a spectator to cock fights. Who could say whether this early exposure to such violence cultivated a bloodthirst in Luke?

Outside of close family members and a tight-knit group of church folks, the Chang family didn't socialize much. Even the cousins they occasionally hung out with were distant ones. Leah's only memory of her maternal grandmother, Doris, was visiting her once and being served potato salad with too much mayonnaise in it. And the children's occasional visits with Jay's mother were always hampered by the language barrier as Leah and Luke did not speak Hmong and their paternal grandmother did not speak much English.

Heidi was determined to keep her children away from the tempting influences of a sinful world. "Because of the way we were raised, we didn't make friends easily. Even at church, there were cliques. Most of the time we were on the outside of those groups," Leah recalled.

The siblings weren't allowed to go to the movies, to school dances, to roam the mall aimlessly, or to attend local football or basketball games. They were under the relentless supervision of their mother 24/7. Heidi's zealous protection of her children was consistent throughout Luke and Leah's childhood, with one glaring exception: Heidi invited her father, Gene Dale Lincoln, into their home following his release from prison.

According to the Michigan Department of Corrections, Gene was released from prison on July 4, 1985. He served the very minimum he could serve under his sentence—ten years for the murder of the young coed Nancy Laws and for sexually assaulting her post-mortem. A total of ten years for one murder and for the attempted abduction of twelve-year-old Doni Heuss, who likely would have ended up dead had she not fought him off.

Despite his crimes, Heidi had kept in touch with her father over the years, before and after his release. Luke and Leah had never had any contact with Gene until Heidi told them one day that their grandfather was going to be moving to North Carolina. "Up until that time, I'd never had a grandpa, so I was really excited to have him around," Leah said.

What Gene did between the time he was released in 1985 and the time he moved to North Carolina is a mystery. During the ten years he'd been imprisoned, the teen he abducted at Hungerford Lake had grown into a young woman, close to the age Nancy Laws was when Gene murdered her. Yet the Michigan Department of Corrections never bothered to notify Doni Heuss that her abductor was being released. "Many things were hidden from me back then," Doni said. However, she does remember getting a strange phone call about the time of Gene's release, a phone call that has haunted her all these years.

The Chang family met Gene at the bus station. There was much excitement over this welcoming of a family member the children didn't even know they had—their mother's father. The children knew their father's father had been killed in war, but there was no mention of their mother even having a father until they learned he was coming to stay with them for a while. Introductions were made, pleasantries exchanged, handshakes and hugs all around. When they returned to their home, Leah ran to her room and gathered up some of her Little Golden Books and brought them to her grandfather. Handing them over to Gene, Leah and Luke scooched in close to see the pictures of *Pokey Puppy* as Gene read the story of the dog who always got left out of everything. Gene read a couple of more stories to his grandchildren before Heidi intervened.

"That's enough," Heidi said. "Your grandpa has had a long trip. He's tired." She picked up the books and handed them to Leah. "Put these back in your room." Pouting, Leah reluctantly took the books as she and Luke bid their grandfather goodnight.

If Heidi had any compunction about allowing her father near her children, she never said. Instead, Jay and Heidi told the kids, Luke, six, and Leah, four, that their grandfather would be living with them until he got a place of his own.

Leah has no memory of Heidi ever speaking ill of Gene. Whatever Heidi knew about the murder and rape of Nancy Laws, she kept to herself. If she knew about the abduction of the strong-hearted Doni Heuss, Heidi never spoke of it to her children. Not even after her own son was arrested for murder. Leah claims she doesn't know to this day why her grandfather was in prison. She says that neither she nor Luke has ever known what crimes their grandfather committed, but her statement doesn't quite square with certain facts. Like when Heidi gave her testimony at church in order to drum up financial support, she spoke to the life she had led as a young girl, raised up in a home with an alcoholic mother and a father imprisoned for murder.

Who can say why Leah felt the need to deny knowing about the crimes of her grandfather? Obviously, she had heard her own mother's testimony on those fundraising visits to churches. Did she never ask her mother, "Who was it Grandaddy killed?" Or was Leah being untruthful because she thought it might somehow protect Luke to pretend that there weren't two murderers from the same family?

If there is a connection between the murder Gene committed and those that his grandson would go on to commit decades later, few in the family are willing to talk about it. Contacted at his home in North Carolina, Gene's son, Lewis, said, "Our situation needs to be studied by science and psychiatric experts if any benefit is to come from this tragedy. If you want to help, pass it off to someone who can figure out what caused it."[2]

There are people trying to do just that, I assured him.

CHAPTER THIRTEEN

Luke joined the Marines straight out of high school. It was Heidi's idea, an idea that didn't set well with Jay or Leah. Neither of them considered Luke a good fit for the Marines. Leah figured she was better suited for the Marines than her brother.

"When I was five, my dad took me and Luke, who was seven at the time, out into the woods behind our house. Dad's intent was to teach us gun safety and how to shoot the family's .22 rifle. I hit dead center three times out of three shots. Luke completely missed two shots and almost missed the last one. I've always been a better shot than my brother, until he joined the Marines. Although he will never admit that."

It had always been assumed that Luke, the smart one in the family, would go to college. In preparation for that, Heidi bent her own strident rules and enrolled Luke and Leah in a private Christian school. New Manna Christian School is located along a lonesome stretch of North Carolina's highway in a town littered with economic hardship. Located off Marion's main thoroughfare of Court Street, New Manna sits on a grassy rise behind New Manna Baptist Church, which bills itself as a Bible-believing (King James Version) fellowship that is "old-fashioned, Independent Baptist." The church runs a very active bus ministry that reaches beyond Marion. There is a dozen or more buses in the parking lot between the school and the church.

Leah had long wished for an opportunity to expand her lame social life. She'd made a few friends at church but claimed she was never allowed to join them at football games, or to hang out at the mall on a Saturday, or grab a pizza with them on a Friday night. But it was not Leah's desire for a more active social life that compelled Heidi to relinquish some control over her children. It was a more practical matter. Luke was a senior, and most of the colleges and universities at that time would not accept the homeschool degree that he was earning under his mom's tutelage. He would either have to earn a GED or a diploma from an accredited high school. New Manna offered that accreditation.

Leah, a junior, was thrilled about attending New Manna. She possessed her father's easygoing and good-natured demeanor. Still, it was hard at first. Both she and Luke were uncomfortably shy and socially awkward, Luke even more so than Leah. Talking came easier for her, and she was hungry for friendship. Conversely, Luke, faced with uncomfortable social situations, retreated further into a world of books and intellectual endeavors, the place he was most confident.

While she was a junior at New Manna, Leah cultivated her first real friendship, a girl named Irena. "We were lost without each other. We were really good friends," Leah recalled. For the very first time, Leah had someone outside her family she could talk with, laugh with, be a girl with. But Luke was lost at New Manna. Socially inept and intellectually superior, he remained an outcast, the kind of forgettable character that passes through the hallways of every high school in every corner of this nation. Luke possessed a vivid inner life but failed to build any lasting friendships. He was not quick-witted enough to break into the cliques that were long-established at New Manna. It had to bother him, but Luke just let on like he didn't care.

One afternoon, passing from one class to the next, Leah eyed Luke sitting on a bench in the school's entryway. He had all his books with him.

"What's going on?" Leah asked, concerned that her brother might be sick.

Avoiding eye contact, Luke answered, "I'm headed home."

"Why?" Leah asked.

"Don't worry about it," Luke snapped.

That evening at home, Leah was barred from a conversation between her brother and her parents. She knew her mother was upset with her brother, but she had no idea why. "I could hear raised voices, heated speaking. Mom was huffing and puffing around a lot," Leah said.

A week passed—a week in which Luke was not at school—before Jay confided to his daughter that the principal at New Manna had expelled her brother.

"Expelled? Why?" Leah was sure that if Luke had been in a fight, she would have heard about it. Maybe Luke was disrespectful to a teacher. He could be surly that way at times. She'd seen him be that way with their mom on occasion. Heck, she was that way with their mom on occasion. The older the kids got, the more Heidi could feel her control slipping away, and it frightened her. Had she done enough to prepare them for the world? To keep them out of harm's way?

"He hacked into a teacher's computer," Jay replied.

Leah didn't ask any more questions. She didn't want to know if her brother had hacked into the computer to change a grade or to look at porn. What did it matter? As bright as he was, Luke made dumb decisions sometimes. Leah marked this up to one of Luke's more stupid choices. Boys. Such lamebrains at times.

Leah spent the next few weeks trying to fly below the radar, steering clear, especially of her mom. Luke spent a lot of time alone in his room. Every now and then, Jay's anger would surface, and he'd speak sharply to Luke. That was about the extent of the anger expressed within the household. Silence or sharp words. Some huffing and puffing, some sulking around, but mostly a discordant silence fell over the Chang household. Everyone understood that expulsion was not the only reckoning for Luke's misdeed. The real reckoning would affect his entire future. As Jay and Heidi saw it, Luke had just blown any shot he had at all at getting into college.

There would be no scholarships, and without scholarships, there would be no college. The family simply could not afford it. Their bright hope would not be earning a college degree any time soon. Luke would need to carve out a different path, and he would have to do it quickly, given that he was a senior and no further education loomed on his horizon.

Heidi was the one who made the decision. "The best thing for you now is to join the military," she said. "It's really the best career path remaining. They will accept a homeschool diploma. Nobody else is going to."

Jay wasn't fully on board with Heidi's plan. He thought that Luke could probably get into a community college, work and pick up a few classes while he grew up a little, learned the error of his ways. The military held little appeal to Jay, given the family's history. Jay's father was one of the jungle guerillas of Vietnam who had fought alongside the Americans and had lost his life in the process. "My dad didn't want to see his son go to war and possibly lose him, too," Leah explained.

For her part, Leah didn't want her brother to go off someplace—God only knew how far—where she might not get to see him but once or twice a year. Luke was the one constant companion of her entire life, her first and only truly close friend. Without her brother by her side, Leah wasn't sure who she was, who she would become.

But Heidi was adamant. The military would accept a homeschool diploma. The military would make a man out of Luke. The military would not tolerate any foolishness. In many ways, the military was a good substitute for the religion Heidi practiced. It provided structure, demanded obedience, honored traditions, and ensured strict oversight. The very same sort of oversight Heidi practiced.

What could possibly go wrong?

CHAPTER FOURTEEN

Casey Lee Byrams was everything Luke Chang was not.[1] Raised up in the foothills of North Alabama, Casey was a country boy through and through. He could have passed as a younger version of Jimmy Kimmel, both in demeanor and good looks. Making people laugh and having a good time was Casey's jam. It is almost impossible to find one photo of Casey in which he isn't smiling or laughing. Casey, a twin, was tall, dark, and handsome. He had the thick hair of a TV evangelist. He usually kept it pushed to one side or stuffed up underneath a ball cap.

His natural charm and engaging nature drew people close. Peers felt better about themselves simply because Casey regarded them as his confidant. He loved without reservation and embraced everyone as a friend. A gifted musician, Casey envisioned himself the next American Idol. "Casey got his first guitar at age fourteen. He taught himself to play by ear," his mother Charlotte recalled. "Eventually, he became that kid who could play anything. He would tell me he was going to play a little ditty. I would tell him not to play it again until he learned the whole thing. And he would!"

Book learning was not Casey's gig. Never had been. The whole point of school for Casey was the social interaction it provided. He could infuriate teachers one minute and charm them the next. That was a trait that he would carry with him for the rest of his short life. He despised taking tests, writing essays, but loved writing songs and creating story through verse. It's difficult to meet anyone in Casey's hometown of Cullman, Alabama, who isn't a natural-born storyteller. Casey was no exception.

Cullman is located about an hour's drive north of Birmingham, too far and much too important to be a bedroom community. The former Cherokee stomping grounds became the home for German immigrants in the late 1800s. Less than twenty thousand in population, Cullman has turned out more than its fair share of successful folks—Big Jim Folson, former governor of Alabama; designer Charles Kleibacker; nationally acclaimed chef James Stitt; actor Channing Tatum; athletes Zac Tubbs, Josh Rutledge, Wayne Trimble; musicians Holly Williams (daughter of Hank Williams, Jr.) and JoJo Billingsley.

Downtown Cullman is home to the internationally recognized Southern Accents Architectural Antiques, one of the nation's premier salvage and restoration businesses. There's a story locals tell over at Berkley Bob's Coffeehouse that the former NBC news anchor Katie Couric once called Garlan Gudger, now a state senator and owner of Southern Accents, and told him she wanted to visit his store on a Sunday after dropping her daughter at space camp in nearby Huntsville. Garlan, a congenial and hospitable fella, reportedly told Katie Couric that he was sure sorry, but he couldn't open the store for her on a Sunday because that was the Lord's Day and they didn't open for nobody on that day. Of course, the truth is Garlan had no idea who Katie Couric was, or he might have reconsidered.[2]

That's the kind of community Casey Byrams grew up in—a town where people might not know your name, but they will speak to you anyway, and quite possibly buy you a cup of coffee at Berkeley Bob's if you are willing to swap stories with them.

Casey's parents, Paul and Charlotte, also grew up in the area. Charlotte was number ten of eleven kids. In parts of Alabama, it's a sign of pride to be raised up hardscrabble. It means you are a survivor. The Byrams did not have health insurance when a sonogram at six months revealed Charlotte was pregnant with twins. Both babies were breach, which meant Charlotte might need a C-section. "The hospital wanted us to give them $800 a month to prepay for the births," Charlotte said. "We didn't have it." Charlotte was advised to drop in to her local county hospital when she went into labor. She would not be turned away even if she couldn't pay.

The night before Casey and his twin sister Lacy were born, Paul borrowed money from his daddy for gas so he could drive his wife to the hospital. The healthy babies arrived within minutes after Charlotte was wheeled in. "We pawned a gold necklace to buy the required car seats to bring them home," Charlotte recalled.

There was no nursery, no bassinettes, no cribs awaiting their babies. Just two cardboard boxes beside a sleeper sofa. "I was embarrassed at the lack of the nursery as our small-town neighbors and relatives came to our single-wide trailer to see them. But they grew up just fine in those little boxes."

Lacy and Casey grew up not only as womb siblings but as friends. Much the same as Leah and Luke had. The other thing Casey and Luke had in common was their motivation for enlisting in the Marine Corps: they'd both gotten into trouble, Luke for hacking into a teacher's computer, Casey for drug use. The two Marine recruits, who were from different zip codes and different moral codes, were assigned to be roommates in Biloxi, Mississippi. While other Marines were deploying to Iraq or Afghanistan, Casey and Luke were sent to Kessler Air Force Base.

Casey was happy about being stationed in Biloxi. Although it was a half-day's drive to Cullman, it was much closer to home than his basic training at Parris Island, SC. The best part of all? Kessler was within driving distance of his girlfriend Megan Keel.

Megan and Casey met the summer of 2008 at a mutual friend's party.[3] At the time, Casey was a wayward twenty-year-old, aimlessly drifting post–high school. He possessed the restless soul of a creative. Casey might have very well set off for a big career in Nashville, writing and performing, had he had a mentor to help him along or just caught that lucky break. It was a dream of his.

Megan, an only child, was a sophomore at Cullman High. She was bright but not studious, pretty but not in a flamboyant way; she was a sublime country-girl pretty. Casey couldn't help but notice her across the room. Megan was peeved at a fellow who was hitting on her. Casey moseyed over, slung his arm over Megan's shoulder in a stake-your-claim move, and spent the rest of the evening protecting her from further unwanted advances. Megan was smitten from that moment on. "I thought he was charming," she said. "He was so full of cheer and excitement. It was amazing to see how much happiness he brought to other people. He just had so much charisma and good vibes."

Megan's parents were divorced. When she and Casey hooked up that summer, Megan was living with her mom. If her mother had any reservations about Megan dating a boy four years older, she kept those concerns to herself. Her mom appeared as charmed by Casey as Megan was. "Casey didn't know I was sixteen until he went to meet my mother. She was the one who told him my age. Casey told my mom he was twenty, but my mother is more a judge of character than anything else, so the four-year gap didn't bother her. She thought Casey was very respectful. She fell in love with him. He was so sweet to her. He became my best friend. I was ready to be with him forever."

Neither of Megan's parents knew anything about Casey's drug abuse. When Megan met Casey, he was doing his best to stay clear of the marijuana, meth, cocaine, whatever other substances had dogged him in the past. Megan marked Casey's drug abuse as a willingness to try new things. She was too young then to consider that Casey had more of an addictive personality than merely an adventuresome one.

The couple spent most everyday of that summer together. When Casey left for basic training in August, Megan returned to high school. They didn't see each other again until December. That time apart intensified their desire for one another. When Casey got stationed to Biloxi in January of 2009, Megan was overjoyed. Life was going to be so much sweeter with Casey within driving distance.

CHAPTER FIFTEEN

As soon as Casey returned to Alabama from basic training, he gave Megan a promise ring and told her that he wanted to spend his forever with her. For now, though, the two would have to settle for every other weekend in Biloxi. Not surprisingly, Megan's mom wasn't keen on the idea of her daughter driving back and forth to Mississippi alone. "I had to call her every hour from the road until I got there," Megan said. "Once she knew I was with Casey, she was fine."

Casey had warned Megan ahead of her first trip to Mississippi that his new roommate was kind of an oddball, but Megan didn't meet Luke Chang until her third trip to Biloxi. Right away, she observed that Casey and Luke were complete opposites. Luke was rigid, controlled, a follow-the-rules kind of fellow, whereas Casey lived to challenge the rules. "Casey was a free, artistic spirit," Megan said. "He wasn't a neat freak like Luke. Luke would get upset because Casey kept the room so messy. Luke would clean it and get after Casey for not doing his part to keep it clean. Casey would just laugh at him." Luke was reserved, but when upset, he could be a bit of a nag. Megan thought that an unusual trait in a fellow as young as Luke.

There were other things that Megan learned about Luke during those trips, like the fact that Luke didn't drink, ever, and didn't smoke pot. He had never had a girlfriend, and according to Casey, Luke had never had sex. Casey speculated that Luke probably had never even kissed a girl. By itself, growing up in a religious household as Luke had is not necessarily an unusual thing in the Bible Belt, but Luke's upbringing was far more strident than anything Megan or Casey had encountered previously. "I thought he was a little strange," Megan said. "Luke seemed very innocent, nerdy, I guess. I thought it was odd that he was in the Marines because of his character and how religious he was."

The Marines can be hard on a person. Even Casey, who hadn't exactly led a sheltered life, had changed. The Marines made Casey more hard-edged, as if he had lost a part of that tenderness that had prompted him to come to her aid that first night they met. "After Basic, Casey was a different person. He lost something. His happiness. He wasn't the same person I had fallen in love with. It was really bizarre," Megan recalled.

For his part, Casey was proud of having accomplished something difficult. The Corps gave Casey a sense of identity and brotherhood. Outside the Marines, Casey was the kid with a drug problem. Inside the Marines, he was the enlistee who made boot camp bearable for others. Employing irreverent wit, Casey could make the most hardened sergeant break into fits of laughter. Most Marines learn pretty quickly to keep their thoughts and their emotions to themselves. Not Casey. The artist in Casey valued emotions. Feelings fueled his music, his creativity. The Marines would demand a lot from him, but Casey stubbornly held onto the creativity within.

"Casey picked the Marines because of the dress blues," Megan said. "He thought they were the most gorgeous things he'd ever seen. But he had no desire to go to Iraq or Afghanistan. He didn't have an urge to do all that. He didn't want to be separated from his family or deal with all that goes on in a war zone."

Keesler AFB is a training ground for the Air Force, the Navy, and the Marines. The mission of the Marines at Keesler is straightforward: "To provide as a supporting detachment combat ready, entry level Marines that are highly trained within their Military Occupational Specialty to the Marine Air-Ground force."[1] There are four specific Marine schools at Keesler: Spectrum manager, test measurement and diagnostic equipment, general purpose electric test equipment calibration and miniatous, and lastly, Meteorological Oceanographic Analyst forecast. Or, as it's more commonly referred to in the civilian world, weatherman. Casey and Luke studied the latter.

"Casey was constantly telling me what kind of cloud formation was overhead, telling me whether it was going to rain or not. I would get so mad at him because it felt like I was in a science class," Megan said. She laughed over the memory of those luxurious now-faraway days.

It was obvious to Megan and anyone else within earshot at Keesler that Luke possessed a level of smarts that Casey lacked. "You could tell Luke was very smart just by the way he would speak, the words he used," Megan said. "Luke was always reading or playing video games. He would laugh along with others, but he was awkward socially. If he told a joke, it was usually lame. I don't think he had a lot of other Marine friends. Casey was it."

The meteorologist program at Kessler is a nine-month study course. The detachment there is about one hundred Marines or less, so they live in one wing of the barracks—dorm-like rooms with a shared bathroom. There are many amenities on base, including a movie theater, rec center, bowling alley, skate park, running track, baseball field, Chapel, and several fast-food joints. Recruits have options for free time without having to go into town, although Biloxi is hardly a town a Marine would want to avoid. Casey and Megan took every opportunity to explore the city. On occasion, they would invite Luke to join them.

Casey and Luke could not have been more different than if they were a dragonfly and a mole. Casey flitted from one thing to the next, infusing every experience with laughter and adventure. Luke, taught to be wary of outsiders, was cautious in most every way, hanging back, always the silent one in a group. While Casey wanted to soar, Luke sought to burrow. Casey saw it as his mission to educate Luke in the ways of the world. It was a mission he was well-equipped to fulfill.

Yet, over time, the two unlikely roomies developed a friendship based upon mutual need and true affection. It was as if their paths were ill-fated to cross. No one recognized the dangers embedded in their friendship until it was far too late for anyone to intervene.

CHAPTER SIXTEEN

After a couple of months, Megan grew tired of the drive between Cullman and Biloxi. Casey was home once or twice, but most of the travel fell to her. She spent two or three weekends out of every month making the round trip. Desperate to break up the drive's boredom, Megan invited her girlfriend Desiree Speegle to join her. Next to Casey, Desiree was Megan's closest friend.

The girls were classmates at Cullman High School. Their friendship started out rocky over petty jealousies, but the two grew to be best friends during their sophomore year.[1] Megan was popular with the boys before she met Casey. Desiree, on the other hand, was more like Luke, quiet, reserved, almost shy. She was happy to stay in the background, uncomfortable in the limelight. Desiree was every bit as pretty as Megan, but she lacked Megan's natural confidence and infectious ways. Desiree was taller and thinner. Her hair was various shades of blond, from strawberry to platinum, and usually cut in a blunt, chin-length style. Desiree was a keen observer of people, and she possessed a quick wit. Like Luke, she was a good listener, with a tender heart for troubled souls, of which she was one.

Megan's effervescent personality dwarfed Desiree's more quiet nature. Desiree didn't dominate the room the way Megan did. She was guarded, more fragile. From an early age, Desiree had struggled with her health. Megan marked those problems up to an eating disorder, but Desiree suffered from an auto-immune disorder and diabetes. "For some reason the nerves in my stomach stopped working," Desiree said. Her health problems magnified themselves during her high school years. Desiree grew so thin, Megan worried she might die. "I couldn't digest food," Desiree said. "Doctors put me on liquid nutrition, a feeding tube, and a lot of different medications."

Even so, her weight plummeted to eighty pounds. "It was bad," Desiree recalled. "It was hard to date someone like me. I stayed so sick. I couldn't go out like everyone else. Because of the diabetes, I couldn't drink and party like my classmates." At times, her chronic health problems strained her friendship with Megan. It could be difficult to be the close friend of someone with such a severe chronic health condition. There were many times when Desiree's poor health kept her confined to a bed, unable to join Megan or others in the usual high school activities.

Whatever concerns Desiree had about Megan hooking up with Casey—and she did have concerns—she kept to herself. Bossing others just wasn't Desiree's style. She could barely keep her own complicated life together, given she was being raised up by a single mom with limited income and even more limited health insurance. Desiree worried about Megan and Casey. Rumor around Cullman was that the reason Casey joined the Marines was because of some deal he'd cut with a judge over a drug infraction. Desiree worried that her two friends were bad for each other.

Like many of their Alabama peers, Desiree and Megan both smoked weed, although Desiree's diabetes precluded her from too many indulgences. "I would drink sometimes, mostly to fit in," Desiree said. "Everyone would smoke some weed, but it was never to the point of getting shitty and passing out."

Many Alabama lawmen take a much sterner approach to marijuana use than kids getting shit-faced drunk. A possession charge of any sort could land a fellow like Casey in a whole heap of trouble. Still, it wasn't like Casey tried to hide his affinity for pot. Once, Casey even showed Megan the crop growing at home. "I was blown away," Megan said. "I'd never seen something like that. We were at his house, and he said, 'Let me show you something really quick.' There were all these kinds of plants growing. Some small. Some very large. There was special lighting for them. It didn't scare me exactly, but it was shocking. I was only a junior in high school, and I'd never seen anything like that before."

It was a friend from school who first plied Casey with weed, then later, more dangerous substances, Megan said. She was sure that Casey's parents, Paul and Charlotte, knew about Casey's pot smoking. She wasn't sure, however, if it bothered them or not. Paul wasn't in the best of health, and Megan described Charlotte as an "Earth Mother" who was naturalistic in her approach to life. "Charlotte was into all those organic ways of doing things," Megan said. Casey claimed that his mother smoked pot, too, but Megan wondered if Casey was trying to justify his own use by bringing his mom into it. "Back then I thought if his mom smoked weed that was pretty cool," Megan said. "Now, I find it really kind of sad. All Casey's friends knew about it."

Casey was the only one among his siblings who smoked pot. "His sisters didn't. They are just very sweet girls," Megan said. "His oldest sister is the 'churchy type,' very, very sweet. And those girls were number one with their mama. They were perfection."

Although beloved, Casey was a troubled soul. Despite all his charm and natural talents, Casey never felt like he measured up. He hid his insecurities behind laughter, the false bravado, and the proud Marine strut. All of it was just a coverup for the little boy within, the boy who wanted everybody to like him. The boy who wanted most of all to be admired and applauded.

Choosing the Marines may seem like an odd lifestyle for a fellow like Casey. An artist at his core, perhaps he was searching for boundaries that would help his undisciplined nature. It was almost as if Casey was afraid of his own talents, afraid to dream bigger for himself. Could it be that he feared trying and failing? Or was it that he feared trying at all?

Megan wasn't sure what all the demons were that haunted Casey, but she was sure that his drug use was the way in which Casey kept his demons at bay. In those days of young love, nobody had any clue that the very thing Casey used to self-medicate would one day become the very demon that turned on him. No. On those trips back and forth to Biloxi, the girls would cruise up and down the freeway, the radio blasting the tunes of M.I.A.'s "Paper Planes" and singing along:

"Third world democracy

Yeah, I got more records than the K.G.B.

So, uh, no funny business . . .

All I wanna do is

And take your money."

Megan nor Desiree had any notion how prophetic those lyrics would become.

CHAPTER SEVENTEEN

It was Casey's idea to set Luke up with Desiree.

"You are both virgins," Casey teased Luke. "You should hook up."

Casey didn't really know whether Desiree was a virgin or not. He and Desiree had a fun-loving but sometimes cranky relationship. They'd bonded over their devotion to Megan, but it was also a source of contention for them. Casey was possessive, and he was particularly so of Megan. Having Desiree hook up with Luke would allow Casey to monopolize his time with Megan. He resented sharing what precious time he had with Megan with anyone else, even Desiree.

On occasion, when he felt safe enough, Luke would explain to Casey and Megan that it was his faith in Jesus Christ that kept him from drinking, smoking, cussing, and having sex outside of marriage. If his fundamentalist upbringing had taught him anything, it was to follow the rules, to not stray outside the lanes. Besides, it was beneficial to his fellow Marines that Luke didn't drink. He was the designated driver when they all went out, and because Luke didn't smoke or drink, he had a lot more expendable income, which he was always willing to share with Casey. It was the Christian thing to do, right? While many of his fellow Marines were blowing nearly every penny they made, Luke was stashing it. Or at least he was when Casey wasn't bumming it off him.

That Casey was using Luke was evident to everyone, including Luke. Sometimes, he would complain about it to Desiree, but not much. "Luke had a lot of money in savings," Desiree said. "He paid for everything." Paying for drinks or motel rooms for Casey and Megan made Luke feel useful, maybe even wanted. He was brought up under the strictures of being a servant to others, so helping out Casey didn't seem like buying a friendship. It seemed the Christ-like thing to do.

Casey was always quick to include Luke, partly because Casey was a friend to everyone and partly because it served Casey's own purposes. Friendships had eluded Luke, mostly because they were discouraged and frowned upon by his mother. Desiree was the one person Luke cared about intimately. She seemed to instinctively understand what made him such a quirky fellow. It helped that Desiree lived on the margins herself, and that having been raised in northern Alabama, she was familiar with the culture of religious isolationism. This notion of being "set apart from the world."

Parents like Heidi are common within the culture of the church. The more fundamentalist the beliefs, usually the more severe the isolationism. "Me and Luke used to talk about his growing up all the time," Desiree said. "He told me that's why he went into the military, because all his life he had been secluded from the outside world. That's why he's the way he is. It's hard to understand him, but I did. Not interacting with kids his age really made him anti-social. It was hard for him to approach people and not be weird."

Most kids form their first friendships in kindergarten or first grade, but Luke's first true friend was Casey. Luke allowed himself to be used by Casey because he longed for the friendship Casey offered. During those early days in Biloxi, Casey and Luke developed an unhealthy co-dependency upon each other that would ultimately mar their friendship and, in Luke's case, his very life.

Casey used Luke for his money, and Luke used Casey to belong. Had Luke been allowed, encouraged even, to develop healthy friendships growing up, he might not have been so easily manipulated by Casey. The very thing that Heidi tried so desperately to protect her son from—the enticements of the world—were the very things Casey introduced Luke to. It was Casey who persuaded Luke to start drinking. It was Casey who convinced Luke to get matching SEMPER FI tattoos on their forearms. It was Casey who encouraged Luke to hook up with Desiree. It was Casey who reportedly hired a hooker to get Luke laid for the first time. It was Casey who taught Luke to laugh at himself, to loosen up, and to enjoy life. And life had never been more enjoyable for Luke than in those early years with Casey.

CHAPTER EIGHTEEN

I n January of 2010, their Low Altitude Air Defense (LADD) program at Biloxi abruptly ended. Casey claimed to have passed his tests for the LADD program but he was charged with cheating. He told Megan he hadn't cheated, but no matter, the Marines had enough evidence of cheating to keep him from finishing the program. Luke was out, too, although it's unclear if he failed it so he could be transferred with Casey.

Both men were reassigned to Fort Bliss, Texas, where they were handed over to Gunnery Sergeant Thomas Joyce.[1] A model Marine, Sgt. Joyce would be their instructor for most of their classes during their time in Texas. Sgt. Joyce wasn't that much older than either of the recruits, but he was a professional who took his duty with a sober-minded approach both Luke and Casey lacked. Shortly prior to his transfer to El Paso, Casey underwent surgery for a hip fracture. Megan recalled that Casey had two major health setbacks in Mississippi—the hip fracture and a knee injury. These physical issues and Casey's propensity for the party life had put his military career in jeopardy. When he arrived at Fort Bliss, Casey was overweight and out of shape. It was Sgt. Joyce's job to rebuild Casey into a specimen of steel, capable of fighting alongside the nation's finest. The good sergeant clearly had his work cut out for him.

"I would drop by the barracks and find Casey hiding Domino's pizza and two liters of Mountain Dew or Dr. Pepper under his bed. Casey would laugh and say he was sorry for being such a fat ass," Sgt. Joyce said. The sergeant would laugh along, but then he would make Casey go for a ten-mile run, a run they would do together. "If I was going to make him go, I was going to go with him," Sgt. Joyce said. For a professional Marine like Sgt. Joyce, leading requires action. He couldn't very well require something of Casey he wasn't willing to do himself: "You have to be willing to devote your time to your men."

Fortunately for Sgt. Joyce, devoting time to Casey was a part of the job he relished. From the first moment they met, the sergeant took a liking to the Cullman kid with the musical bent. "When we first met, Casey had a pen in hand and was drumming out a beat on his desk and singing some tune he was working on. Casey said he wished he'd brought his guitar with him." He had left his guitar behind at the family home in Alabama. "I knew his world," Sgt. Joyce said. "Casey reminded me of Bradley Nowell from Sublime. He expressed himself best through music." So Sgt. Joyce lent Casey his own guitar and told him he could use it while he was in Texas. From then on out, whenever Casey wasn't in class or at work, he was in his room with that guitar or sitting on a bench somewhere picking out a tune.

At that time, Sgt. Joyce taught twenty-one of the thirty-two classes new recruits took at Fort Bliss—everything from how to handle a machine gun to what to do in live-fire situations. In addition, he had overnight duty at the barracks every four days. While he served as a mentor to anyone he taught, he had an especially tight relationship with Casey. "Students like him bring a breath of fresh air, breaking up the monotony of the job. Casey made everything fun and different. He made you think. He made you laugh. He made you happy just to be around him," Sgt. Joyce recalled.

However, Sgt. Joyce did not form that kind of relationship

with Luke. "I was aware that Casey was friends with Luke, but our relationship was strictly instructor to student." For the most part, Joyce found Luke to be unremarkable. "He focused on his studies. He appeared to be a normal young guy. No signs of any kind of anger or angst." There was nothing that would give Joyce pause or cause him to question whether Luke would make a worthy Marine or not. "Out of the classes I taught, I would recognize most of those guys. A handful of them I would know by name. But Luke wasn't one of those that you would always remember."

In many ways, Luke was simply forgettable, whereas Casey was unforgettable. Luke tried not to call attention to himself, whereas Casey lived for the spotlight. In retrospect, Joyce said, "Luke was fairly selective with the people he interacted with. Casey had a core group of people around him, and I was aware that Luke was in that core group, but he guarded himself from everybody."

Sgt. Joyce is a Marine loyalist who believes that the Marine Corps is first and foremost family. His entire methodology of instruction is to get new recruits to think first about the welfare of their fellow Marines. While the skill of killing another human being is part of the preparation for all Marines, Joyce pointed out that "we don't train people to be homicidal." Neither Casey nor Luke were the type of people that Joyce would peg as future murderers. "We train to conduct business and kill if necessary to protect the Marine Corps family, but that's it." Joyce is particularly sensitive to the notion of the military making killers out of young men and women. His own father was murdered when Joyce was a young boy.

For Sgt. Joyce, a career in the military is all about being the sort of person trained to do the honorable thing. Doing the right thing is the dictum he lives by and the dictum he sought to instill in each of the Marines he mentored. Casey, for all his demons, seemed to grasp that, and Luke gave Joyce no reason to suspect that he didn't.

Still, at his core, Casey really had no desire to be far from Cullman, Alabama. What looked like a small-town life to outsiders contained all the life Casey needed or desired: A truck. A gun. A guitar. A dog. A good woman at his side. His sisters and his mama Charlotte nearby. Casey didn't really need much more than that. He had not joined the Marines to get pushed around, bullied; yet it seemed he was getting demeaned daily in El Paso.

"They were making his life miserable," Megan said. "Some of the Marines, who ranked higher, would get shovels of dirt and throw it on the floor Casey had just cleaned and order him to clean it again. They would assault him, pushing those pins he wore into his chest. They would make fun of him, make him feel worthless." Those close to him knew that Casey struggled with depression. The abuse he suffered resurrected Casey's feelings of unworthiness. "He had lost his happiness," Megan said. "He wasn't the same person I had fallen in love with. It was like a switch from night and day. It was bizarre."

Sgt. Joyce was unaware of the abuses Casey suffered at the hands of others. No recruit wants to be the whiner. So Casey kept all that bottled up, bitching about it during the brief phone calls he had with Megan. However, Casey did confide in Sgt. Joyce that he was having troubles with Megan, who was in her senior year of high school. The distance between the two was wearing on Casey, who found it difficult to deal with the loneliness. He didn't like being separated from Megan. He worried that his being in Texas might make her vulnerable to the affections of others. The distance between them was too far for an afternoon drive home.

Trained in suicide prevention, Sgt. Joyce knew not to minimalize the hurt Casey was enduring. Relationship problems are common in every branch of the military. The stress of deployments, separations, constant moves, and the demands of daily life puts untold strains on the best of relationships. Casey not only divulged his girlfriend problems, he told Joyce about his past drug abuse problems as well. While the Marines tested regularly for drug use, there were substances that were considered too inconsequential to test for, substances that, unlike marijuana, did not register on the pee test administered by the Marines at that time. And maybe because of that, because not even the Marines considered it a drug to be leery of, Casey saw no harm in substituting his old cocaine high with the newest thing on the market—Spice.

Spice, also commonly referred to as K2, is a synthetic cannabis that began to appear on the market in 2008. It had quickly gained in popularity by the time Casey and Luke arrived at Fort Bliss. One military spouse from Fort Bliss described her own experience with Spice to *Borderzine* this way: "I thought it was just people exaggerating about the side effects and how strong it was. Everything was moving so slow. After about three minutes, I started panicking because I could feel my heart beating fast, and I couldn't calm myself down. That was the last time I ever touched Spice."[2]

Spice was legal and marketed as a "safe" and "natural" alternative to marijuana. It could be bought at convenience stores, gas stations, and even online. A soldier could run out to the nearest 7-11 and pick up a Slurpee and a package of Spice. No one seemed to know any better. Now, of course, the Drug Enforcement Agency experts have concluded that Spice is two hundred times more powerful than marijuana, often adversely affecting the brain and other internal organs, which can and too often does have an impact on a user's mental health. But at that time, few were aware of the dangers it posed.

It would be hard to determine if Casey's depression was solely the result of problems between him and Megan or if it was a side effect of Spice. Sgt. Joyce could not have made that assessment then, anyway, since he had no clue that Casey was using Spice. "Casey was artistic and expressive. When he got down about something, he left himself vulnerable. There's a tricky side to artistic people like Casey, like Kurt Cobain," Sgt. Joyce said. "I knew he was upset about things between him and his high school sweetheart. I tried to remind him that there were other fish in the ocean."

Besides, Joyce dealt with far more troubling issues than what was going down between Casey and Megan at the time. He had a full-time job trying to keep new recruits from marrying every local stripper they happened upon. No matter what was troubling Casey, he could usually pick up that guitar Joyce loaned him and write a tune to help him wrestle his demons: "My mind is lost; my soul has been poisoned . . . I'm going crazy, spinning out of control," Casey sang. "I've got no chance, no hope for escape. My path has been chosen; my role has been picked."

Hearing the song now, it's almost as if Casey had a premonition of the troubles to come, not just for him, but for Megan, Desiree, and so many others whose names were yet unfamiliar to him. So much evil would follow that it seems a cruel cosmic joke that this Alabama talent and his North Carolina sidekick would ever be stationed at a place named Bliss.

CHAPTER NINETEEN

Once they finished their stint at Fort Bliss, Casey and Luke were given their next orders—Camp Pendleton. The legendary base is regarded by Marines of all ranks as the West Coast's premier duty station, located in Oceanside, California, halfway between LA and San Diego. Beaches. Bikinis. Surfers. Ocean breezes. Civilization. It was almost as if they were being rewarded for doing their time in hot-as-hell Texas and Mississippi. There was only one major roadblock: California was way too far from Cullman. Casey wouldn't be popping home for a weekend the way he did while stationed at Biloxi. The relationship with Megan was already strained by separation. Casey couldn't imagine what would happen if he went to California and Megan stayed in Alabama. Or maybe he could, and it terrified him.

The couple had been planning to marry since Casey gave Megan that promise ring. Casey did not put a lot of planning into the engagement. There were no embraces on a Jumbotron, no billboards along the freeway declaring Casey's love for Megan. There wasn't even an engagement party with beer and a bonfire and high school friends. Just a small diamond ring and Casey's declaration that he wanted to be with Megan forever, so would she marry him? Megan didn't hesitate to say yes: "Casey was my best friend."

On December 21, 2010, during Christmas break, Casey and Megan drove to the Cullman County Courthouse and got married. Casey's momma Charlotte took pictures. Megan doesn't own a single photo from her own wedding day. The couple honeymooned at two- and three-star motels as they made the drive from Alabama to California. For both, it was the adventure of their young lives, seeing the country as they sang along to Taylor Swift's "Love Story": *Romeo, take me somewhere we can be alone. I'll be waiting. All that's left to do is run. You be the prince and I'll be the princess. This love is difficult, but it is real.*

Like most adventures, the beginning was the best part. Neither Megan nor Casey had any idea how expensive setting up a household in Southern California could be, especially the married life of the enlisted. With an estimated thirty-seven thousand active-duty military personnel in the Camp Pendleton area, demand for affordable housing was high. Rent for a one-bedroom apartment averaged about $1,700-$2,000 a month. Far and above the rental market in Cullman, Alabama, where a trailer on the back forty with a lake nearby might cost a person $600 a month. Fortunately, they found a two-bedroom apartment off-base for $1,400 a month. Megan's dad loaned them the money to get settled.

The couple bought an air mattress that served as their bedroom suite. Casey and Megan cobbled together the rest of their household from garage sales and Craigslist's castoffs. As an only child, Megan had never wanted for much. She didn't know what it meant to do without. At home, the fridge was always well-stocked, her clothes closet the same. She worked when she wanted to, not because she needed to. Budgeting was something neither she nor Casey had any experience with.

Like a lot of young married couples trying to survive on a soldier's meager pay, there were weeks that stretched out longer than the paycheck. Eggs had to be counted to see if they would last until payday. Noodles became a staple. Pizza delivery was a luxury item. The lack of money didn't stress Casey the way it did Megan. He was more familiar with money being tight. He had done without before. "He was so optimistic," Megan said. "He said we'd look back and laugh about it someday, but it was emotional for me."

It wasn't just the lack of money; it was the lack of anything familiar. She'd grown up in a community where people knew her, knew her mom and her dad. And Megan had never lived away from Cullman or her parents. The only traveling she had done on her own were the trips she'd made to see Casey. At Camp Pendleton, Megan was just another homesick military spouse in a town full of homesick military spouses. "We were so far away from home," she said. "At home, if I didn't have something, I could walk across the street and borrow it from somebody. But in California, I didn't know anybody." On those days, when it all seemed too much to handle, Megan would take a walk on the beach or go for a drive. She'd tell herself that at least she and Casey were doing this hard thing together. "And that's all that mattered in the long run," she said. Or so she assumed.

It's difficult to hang on to those lies we tell ourselves when the cupboards are bare and the only thing left in the fridge is four eggs and two beers. "We were pretty flat broke," Megan said. It was one of the things that concerned Megan's dad when he made a trip out to Camp Pendleton to visit his daughter in her new environs.

Keith Keel was happy when Megan married Casey. He liked the way Casey was always deferential to others, referring to Keith or other adults with "no, sir" or "yes, sir." Keith thought that showed good manners. "Casey was a super nice guy," Keith recalled. "A real gentle guy." He also respected that Casey really loved his daughter. "Casey always told me that 'if Megan and I aren't together, I'll commit suicide.'" Some parents might have been alarmed that a young man would make such a statement. It might be indicative of obsession, or power and control, but Keith didn't take it that way. He figured that was just Casey's way of declaring how much Megan meant to him. And as her father, Keith appreciated Casey's devotion.[1]

Besides, Keith wanted his daughter to experience all the

adventures of travel that comes with being a military spouse. "I wanted her to see that there was life beyond Cullman. Without an education, she would be stuck in this town making $11 an hour. I thought going to Camp Pendleton would give Megan an opportunity to experience a little bit of life outside of Alabama."

During his brief visit to California, Keith treated his daughter to all the excursions she had not been able to do on her own or with Casey. They visited Los Angeles, drove through Hollywood Hills, and attended one of Hollywood's game shows. They drove on down to San Diego, walked the pier, and marveled over the big ships and the crisp whiteness of the Navy uniforms. They ate out and spent the night at a nice hotel. Megan had forgotten how luxurious a real bed could be. The next day they drove south to Tijuana where they saw men in the back of trucks with machine guns strapped to their chests.

Megan talked about how she'd like to go to college one day, maybe study to be a nurse and do something bigger with her life than just being Casey's wife. Keith liked hearing his daughter talk about her hopes. He encouraged her. "You need to be independent," he said. "Go do what you want to do." The very last thing Keith ever wanted for his daughter was for her life to be dictated by a man— even a good guy like Casey.

When her daddy packed his bag and headed back to his life in Alabama, Megan fell into a funk. She missed her parents, her life in Cullman. Megan found marriage to be more drudgery and longing than she had bargained for. It wasn't that she didn't love Casey as much as it was that she didn't love her life as an enlisted man's wife. Megan hated being strapped financially. Southern California was only glamorous if you could afford the lifestyle that made it so.

It wasn't long after her daddy left that Megan invited Desiree to come live with her and Casey. It wasn't a well-thought-out invitation. "Desiree was crying to me about some issues she was having at home, how she was tired of dealing with everything, so I invited her to come live with us until she could get on her feet," Megan recalled.

At first, Casey thought it a good plan. He liked the idea that Megan, who was terrified of being alone, would have a girlfriend around when he was away on overnight duties. Luke, who was living on base, liked the idea of Desiree moving out to Oceanside, too. He had harbored a crush on Desiree for some time. Casey had teased him over it, but Luke was never one to talk about how he felt. Whenever Casey would prod him, Luke would simply smile and walk off. Still, Casey knew his buddy possessed clear affection for Desiree. Luke's feelings were not reciprocated by Desiree, but she did like the attention. It made her feel good that Luke found her attractive, so she didn't discourage him from flirting with her.

The four of them—Megan, Casey, Luke, and Desiree—were all involved in mutually exploitative relationships. They were young and didn't necessarily realize that they were using each other. Indeed, that didn't cross Desiree or Megan's minds until much later. But by the time it did, it was too late, too much damage had been done, too many bodies lay cold.

CHAPTER TWENTY

Desiree arrived in California on February 21, 2011. She posted the obligatory "in front of palm trees" photo on Facebook. With her then-platinum hair, her shy smile, and her shoulder bag swung over her shoulder in that carefree manner, Desiree could have passed for a vintage Clampett-girl-gone-Hollywood. She wrote, "Sooo this place is nothing like Cullman. I don't think I'll ever go back home." To which Megan replied, "Oh, no your [sic] not. I need my best friend here to get ripped with me." A few days later, Desiree put up another post: "I love California. It's sooo pretty and lovely but the ppl are, well . . . different, lol, no they are straight up fucking weird." A few days later, she posted a photo of Luke at the Waffle House. He's wearing a lopsided smile. He looks as though he'd just woken up, or perhaps he'd never gone to bed.

Desiree had no real plan for creating a life in California. She wasn't sure how long she'd stay. Not having a plan proved to be more wearing on the household than anyone had expected. Should she get a job or not? Should Megan expect her to help with rent or not? How much of Desiree's time was hers, and how much did she owe to Megan? Neither girl could articulate those rising tensions, but those unspoken issues added to the day-to-day drama. "At first having Desiree around was fun," Megan said. "But Casey and I barely had enough money to survive with the two of us. When we added another person, it really created tension. Desiree was a very needy person."

Desiree doesn't recall that time the same way. "Megan held it over my head that it was her apartment, and she could kick me out anytime she wanted." Had there been a plan in place, had there been a timetable for how long Desiree would be staying with the newlyweds, that might have alleviated some of the pressure, but everybody just flew by the seat of their pants. Megan got a part-time job working at McDonalds to make ends meet. Desiree had a more difficult time finding work. "She kept searching for jobs but never found one," Megan said. The truth was Megan suspected Desiree didn't really want to work.

It didn't help matters that there was only one car for the household. Whenever Casey needed a ride to or from base, Megan had to do the fetching. Desiree was dependent upon the couple for pretty much everything: housing, food, rides. All that was a lot of responsibility for Megan, who had never really done much adulting on her own.

When the girls weren't partying, they were fighting. And they weren't the only two fighting. Casey and Desiree had a cockeyed relationship. His jealousy over her friendship with his wife had never really subsided. One minute Casey would jokingly sweep Desiree off her feet, dumping her teasingly head-first into an empty trash can, and the next he would do something mean like take a lighter to her ring finger. Megan would declare Desiree her BFF, and in the next breath, she was throwing Desiree out of her apartment, telling her to get out, find her own place, cussing her up one side and down another.

The only thing consistent in the Oceanside household was the partying. Casey, who had started using Spice in Fort Bliss, was smoking it on a regular basis now. He enticed Megan, then Luke, into using it as well. Desiree, because of her ongoing diabetes, had to be more cautious with her drug and alcohol use. She simply could not afford to indulge in anything to the degree that Casey and Megan did. Not to say she was always the sober one, she was not. When she wasn't posting to Facebook about all the petty tiffs of life, she was putting up posts about how awful she felt after partying too much. One post was a video of a naked Megan in a bathtub, obviously wasted, crying for her daddy, and telling Casey that she didn't trust him, while Casey can be seen laughing and mocking her in return.

The Spice use got out of hand, Megan admitted. "One of Casey's buddies in the Marine Corps had introduced Casey to it, and Casey introduced me to it. He told me it was legal and that nothing was wrong with it. He said it would make me laughy and high. The first time we used it we sat there and laughed so hard. I don't think I've ever laughed as hard at anything in my life. It seems silly now."

Like a lot of drugs, at the onset, Spice seemed harmless. "You could buy it in the store. It was legal," Megan said. "I even knew guys in Cullman who were using it. They were buying it like a jet pack or something. It hadn't hit the news yet that it was making people crazy."

Or killing them. Like a lot of her peers, Megan was an occasional pot user. Nothing near to the degree that Casey indulged in, but she did experiment. Neither she nor Casey were attuned to the addictive nature of Spice. Why should they be? A person could buy all they wanted at the local corner market. "At first, we were using Spice recreationally," Megan said. "Just on occasion. Then more often. And then, before long, we were using it every day, all day, both of us."

It wasn't long before Luke was indulging in it as well. That military life that Heidi imagined would give her son the focus and purpose she thought he needed, as well as the discipline, had mostly bored Luke. He was better read than most of his peers. He knew more history than some teaching it. The structure and routine of the military was not all that different than the rigor of what Luke had grown up with. If there was anything Luke was good at, it was going along to get along. He'd grown up in a household where compliancy was valued and honored. Even joining the Marines was an act of compliance, the accepted retribution for a good son doing wrong.

Few ever stopped to ask Luke what he wanted; what were his dreams for his future? For years, Luke went through life without anyone really knowing him. Books were his escape hatch. As long as he had a book in his hand, he didn't really have to interact with anyone else. Other people, including his parents and Leah, admittedly, left him alone. Did anyone in Luke's life question whether all of his alone time was a problem? Did they ever worry that he was anti-social? It seems Casey was the first person in Luke's life to demand that he come out from behind the books, perhaps the first person who genuinely seemed to really want to know Luke. Desiree was the second, but even she had her own self-interests at heart.

Luke had always been regarded by others as a tender-hearted religious boy from the hollers of North Carolina. "He would give you the shirt off his back," Megan said. "He was quiet and sweet." But his quiet and sweet nature turned to a surly and sullen one after Luke started using Spice on a regular basis.

CHAPTER TWENTY-ONE

On April 11, 2011, Desiree put up a new post on Facebook: *"The person who knows the most about you is the most dangerous person you know."* Shortly afterward, she and Megan flew back to Alabama to collect all of Desiree's belongings and a car so that she could make her move to California more permanent. It was somewhat of a surprising decision considering that Desiree still didn't have a job, and during those few months she'd been in California, Megan had thrown her out of the apartment on several different occasions.

"Megan would kick me out at any time for any reason," Desiree said. "We would always make up, though. She was my best friend, and I understood why she was the way she was. I understood her, but things eventually got so bad in California, I couldn't handle her anymore. It got scary," Desiree said. By "it," she means the instability of all four relationships: Desiree fought with Casey; Casey fought with Megan; Megan fought with Desiree and Casey. Really, the only seemingly stable person in the entire circle of people that they all ran around was Luke. He lived at the barracks during the week and hung around the apartment on the weekends.

The good Christian boy from rural North Carolina underwent a personality change in California. The Marines talk a lot about protecting freedoms. It seemed Luke was finally indulging in some previously denied freedoms. In California, Luke pretty much abandoned most of the good-kid rules he'd grown up with. His mother, Heidi, had it right—bad company does corrupt good character. Luke took up many of the vices Casey espoused. Amused by the transformation in his friend, and perhaps a bit proud of his part in that transformation, Casey once snapped a photo of a very pale Luke sitting on the edge of the bathtub, leaning over the toilet, sick from a night of partying. Casey was apparently pleased about persuading Luke to indulge in drinking and drugging. Did he like that he had brought Luke down to his level? Did it make Casey feel like his addictions weren't all that dangerous if a good kid like Luke was enjoying them, too? There's no way Casey could foretell the lasting effects of his influence over Luke, who had never before had a friend like Casey.

The closer he grew to Casey, the more drinking and drugging he was doing, the more Luke hated living in the barracks. When you live where you work, you begin to feel like the company owns you. You are more slave than freeman. Luke envied Casey's married life, the chance to live off base, and his relationship with Megan. Luke wanted a girlfriend in the worst way. Desiree was an obvious choice. And, although Desiree did not find Luke attractive or desirable, he did possess the one thing she wanted and needed in the worst way: health insurance.

Once Desiree and Megan returned from Alabama, a plan was hatched to address all their needs. Luke and Desiree would marry. The two of them would move in with Megan and Casey. As a military spouse, Desiree would have access to Tri-Care health insurance. As a married man, Luke would be able to get out of the barracks and live off base. And Megan and Casey would have help with rent and living expenses.

Luke and Desiree's marriage would be nothing more than a contractual business deal. "Desiree had been crying about not being able to afford her medical supplies, the ones necessary to manage her diabetes," Megan recalled. "If she married Luke, he could move in with us and we'd all split the rent. Desiree would have insurance and Luke would get extra pay for housing allowance."

It would be a win-win for everybody. Or so they all thought at the time.

"The contract marriage was Megan and Casey's idea," Desiree said. "But in my own selfish ways, I knew I was using Luke. I feel horrible about that now, but he was willing to enter into the contract with me. Had I known it was going to turn into everything that it did, I would have gone back home to Alabama, but I didn't know that then."

On May 11, 2011, Desiree and Luke Chang married in the courthouse in San Marcos. When he was offered the opportunity to kiss his bride, Luke did so with enthusiasm. Desiree claimed it would be the only kiss the two would ever exchange. For her part, marriage was purely an act of desperation. If Desiree had access to health care, she says she never would have married Luke. If she had her own insurance, Desiree wouldn't have needed to exploit Luke the way she did.

None of their families were present for their marriage. Most of Luke's family didn't even know he was getting married. Desiree's mom knew about the marriage, knew it was a ruse designed to cheat a corrupt healthcare system. How could anyone blame Desiree for taking advantage of Luke? Her diabetes was life-threatening. Without the appropriate healthcare, Desiree's life would most assuredly be cut short. Desiree's mom was just thankful Luke was willing to step up and help out. Few, if any, gave thought to how all this might affect Luke emotionally, spiritually, or mentally.

Leah also knew that the marriage was in name only. Luke had told her that much. Leah couldn't imagine marrying somebody under such circumstances. No, she would only marry for love. Still, she wasn't surprised that her brother did. They had both been raised up to care for the less fortunate. The entire family had served in missions overseas. As unorthodox as it might have been, Leah understood this was Luke's way of fulfilling the Gospel of Christ.

Most of Luke's family and peers learned of his marriage when he announced it on Facebook. Heidi was mortified. She couldn't understand why her son married a girl he barely knew. Neither Luke nor Leah warned her that the marriage was purely a business transaction. Desiree was not the girl Heidi or Jay imagined Luke marrying. As far as they knew, Desiree wasn't even a Christian, a prerequisite to them for any marriage.

Heidi wasn't the only one distraught over Luke's announcement. When Desiree saw the Facebook post, she came unglued. She was furious at Luke and told him so. It angered her that her friends might think she loved Luke and that's why she married him. Nothing could be further from the truth. Luke wasn't her type. He would never be her type. The marriage would never be anything other than a legal agreement between two consenting parties. "It wasn't like we were together," Desiree explained. "We'd had several heart-to-hearts about how it would all go down. We had decided that our families could know but not other people. Then Luke went on Facebook and told everyone we were married!"

As soon as she saw the post, Desiree confronted Luke. "What are you doing?" she implored. Silently, she was asking herself a more important question: "What did I get myself into?" Someplace deep within, Desiree knew that it was ridiculous to think any man would marry a woman without expecting something in return. She knew Luke cared for her in ways she would never care for him. But she was in a hard place. Her diabetes was severe. Any job she got wasn't going to pay her medical bills. No insurance is affordable when you are living below the poverty line, and Desiree had lived below that line for most of her young life.

As much as she hated exploiting Luke, Desiree reasoned that he was more than willing to be taken advantage of, so he was just as guilty of using her. "I understood what Luke hoped our marriage would become," she said. "He told me his mom had been in an abusive relationship prior to meeting his dad. His dad stepped in and married her. His mom loved his dad unconditionally because he took care of her. I told Luke, 'This is not what this is.' But I'm not sure Luke saw it any other way."

From the minute Luke bragged on Facebook about being married, Desiree understood she was in over her head. Too late, though. The deed was done. They were married, for better or for worse. Still, she nor anyone else could have ever imagined how much worse things would get. That's the thing about murder, though. Too often it is the result of good intentions gone awry.

CHAPTER TWENTY-TWO

Amyjane Brandhagen had hair the color of autumn maples, and it cupped her face like the hands of a loving friend. She considered herself a klutz, prone to tripping, but her lithe frame lent an elegance to her clumsier moves. A hippie in spirit, she favored tie-dyed shirts, flowered skirts, and walking around barefoot. Her artistic flair drew the admiring attention of strangers and friends alike. She stood apart from the other residents at Goodwin Court Apartments. Amyjane embodied a spirit of openness that drew many into her sphere.

At nineteen, and a year out of high school, Amyjane had moved out on her own. It was time. Yet growing up and paying the bills was harder than she imagined, as she explained to a neighbor. Yvonne didn't know Amyjane all that well. They were both residents at Goodwin Court Apartments on Pendleton's Main Street.

Amyjane had only worked at the Travelodge in Pendleton, Oregon, for a few days, but even that short time frame was long enough for Amyjane to know cleaning hotel rooms was not going to be a job she wanted long-term. Bed-making was the sort of mundane drudgery that Amyjane loathed. She rarely made her own bed. What for criminy sakes was she doing making up the beds of people she didn't know? Money could be a hard-assed master.

Located in the northeast corner of Oregon, Pendleton embraces a cowboy identity. It is home to the internationally known Pendleton Woolen Mills and the Pendleton Round-Up Rodeo. By the time Amyjane graduated from Pendleton High School, the textile mills which bore the town's name were shuttered. Pendleton's economic structure was shifting away from the city's multi-generational white powerbrokers to the ever-expanding Wildhorse Casino at the nearby Native American–controlled land. School enrollment was falling, as were housing prices. Good jobs were harder to come by, especially for those with only a high school education.

One August evening in 2012, as the setting sun cast a rosy glow to the Umatilla River, Yvonne ran into Amyjane on a back stairwell.[1] The river runs through the middle of town, right past the apartment complex. It was a typical summer's eve in Pendleton—warm, dry, a bit dusty from the road dirt blown in by passing cars. Yvonne stopped and asked the new tenant how things were going. Amyjane replied that she had started another part-time job, as a maid at Travelodge.

"That's great," Yvonne said. She knew Amyjane was looking for a job to supplement the one she had at the local Subway shop. Two part-time gigs would enable Amyjane to pay the rent and buy some groceries: the mark of living independent of one's parents.

"I've only worked a couple of days," Amyjane said. "But I'm not sure how long the job will last."

"Why's that?" Yvonne asked.

"The manager thinks I work too slow," Amyjane replied. "He said I was stupid."

"Really? He said that?" Yvonne couldn't imagine any manager would say such a thing to an employee.

"Yeah." Amyjane nodded. "I thought he was going to hit me. He drew his hand back like he was going to."

"Did he? Did he strike you?"

"No."

"You should report him," Yvonne said. "He can't intimidate you like that. For him to even act like he might strike you is wrong."

Amyjane shrugged. "Maybe I just was reading him wrong. He didn't hit me. There was nothing to report. Besides, who would I report him to?"

"If he ever does hit you, you should report him to the police."

"Yeah, okay," Amyjane replied.

"You ought to keep looking for another job."

"Maybe," Amyjane agreed.

Yvonne got the impression that Amyjane was the type of person who would tolerate abuse before she'd report it, even though she appeared to be a confident girl. People don't like to tattle on others, especially when they need the work, which Amyjane did. The whole thing didn't set well with Yvonne. That's what she told the police days later when they came around the apartment asking about Amyjane Brandhagen.

CHAPTER TWENTY-THREE

Luke studied Amyjane from a landing at Pendleton's City Hall. The city library is located directly across the street from the Travelodge, a motel more commonly used by those hoping to save a buck than for business travelers in search of good amenities. There was something about the way the auburn-haired girl moved that reminded him of Desiree. She had the same build as his wife, more angles than curves. She moved with a subaqueous rhythm as if to some internal music. Her autumn-hued hair fell soft against her face like Desiree's, too. Luke watched as Amyjane moved from room to room, pushing a cleaning cart, opening doors, walking head down into the dark caverns of tussled bedsheets and damp towels.

Two months had passed since he'd last seen or even spoken to his wife. Could it have been that long already? Luke checked the date: August 14, 2012. Yes, nearly two months. He hadn't informed Desiree he was leaving. He hadn't spoken to anyone since he'd left: not Desiree, not his sister, not his dad, and certainly not his mother. For all he knew, they might all think him dead.

Who cared if they did? In a way, a part of him had died along with Casey Byrams. He'd learned of Casey's death when Desiree called him at work. He knew something was up when she first called. They'd hardly been on speaking terms as of late. Nervous and upset, Desiree didn't even bother with any calm niceties. Instead, she blurted out her anguish: "Casey's dead!" She was sobbing so hard her words came out in halting gasps.

"What?" Luke replied. He wasn't sure he'd heard her right.

"Casey's dead!" Desiree repeated. "I sent him a text and hadn't heard back, so I checked on Facebook and saw all these posts asking people to pray for his family. I called his momma and she told me. Casey overdosed. He's dead." Casey died on June 7, 2012, in Cullman, Alabama.

Luke was silent.

"I'm going to Alabama," Desiree continued. "You can go with me if you like. I've got to go help Casey's momma, but you'll have to get a ticket back because I'm going to stay for a while."

Desiree and Casey had discussed returning to Alabama together back in April. Casey had wanted to get home in time for Mother's Day. Desiree wanted to go, too, but she'd finally found a job. There was no way she could take time off. She needed the money since she and Luke were on the outs, and he was no longer supporting her.

Casey and Megan had split up months prior after he suspected she was cheating on him. Megan denied all the rumors circulating that she was fooling around with another Marine buddy, but Desiree told Casey it was all true. Casey wasn't sure what to think. He loved Megan, but his regular intake of Spice might have made him more inclined to be paranoid. Casey had long struggled with self-doubt. The thought of Megan cheating on him renewed those insecurities. His drug use didn't help. In fact, it was dirty UAs that finally earned Casey a military discharge. He had been floundering for a very long time.

Luke couldn't have been more shocked if a stranger had gutted him. That's certainly how it felt—like somebody had hollowed him out, carved away all he cared about. He was sick to his stomach. He wanted to puke. He couldn't fathom the reality behind Desiree's words.

Casey dead? Luke would never share another phone call, another toke, another beer with the only friend he'd ever really had. He would never again see Casey pick up a guitar and strum out a tune, and he'd never again hear Casey's volcanic laughter erupt. Luke was looking at a lifetime without Casey.

Rage filled that hollow place within. Rage was always the one emotion Luke felt the most kinship with. There's a power to rage, and Luke liked that power. It filled him up in a way few other things ever did.

"Let me know if you want to go with me," Desiree said, jarring Luke from his mute response. She doesn't even remember if Luke said goodbye or if she just hung up, but she knew he wouldn't go to Casey's funeral. Luke wouldn't ask for the leave time, and even if he did, it wouldn't likely be granted. Casey wasn't a blood relative, and his departure from the Marines had been an unpleasant one. Besides, Desiree was about the last person Luke wanted to make a cross-country road trip with at that point.

Throughout the rest of his workday, Luke moved about stoically, silently grieving. Later that day, he went online and posted the following message on the Facebook memorial page established for Casey:

"At 7:20 this morning, I received the worst news in my life. I was at work when my wife called me with the terrible news. She told me that Casey passed away. This hit me terribly hard. He was like a big brother to me. Looked out for me, kept me out of trouble, and showed me that a person can have fun anywhere, at any time. Even when he was down at his worst, he always tried to put a smile on everyone's face. On my worst day in my worst mood, even when I didn't want to, he could always make me laugh. It was impossible not to. His view on life was this, 'If I can make a person (even a complete stranger I'll never see again) smile, laugh, or feel better about themselves, it just makes my day.' He would go out of his absolute way just to make a person feel at ease or make an awkward situation better. I miss him.

I really miss him a lot. Because of him, I am a Crimson Tide fan (Roll Tide!!). I know he is up in heaven playing his guitar to Jesus. I love you, Byrams, life is a little bit sadder without you, man. – Luke C."

Luke included a photo of Casey that he said was the last one he took of his best friend. In it, Casey wore a T-shirt that read: *I Heart Haters!* Classic Casey. He always believed he could charm his way into the coldest of hearts, and for the most part, he always did.

The message Luke posted on Casey's memorial page was authentic and perhaps the hardest he's ever penned. Luke had long been uncomfortable with emotions. Feelings can be such unruly things; emotions can overtake a person's life and lead them to do the most illogical of acts. Luke didn't like subverting logic to feelings, but from that moment he learned of Casey's death, grief would consume Luke.

The Luke everyone thought they knew got lost.

Literally.

CHAPTER TWENTY-FOUR

The 911 call came at approximately 3:19 p.m. on Tuesday, August 14, 2012. The caller said someone was either "passed out or dead" in a motel room at Travelodge. The 911 operator issued a call for assistance. Pendleton Fire, which was located only a few blocks away, responded swiftly with an ambulance crew.[1]

Kal Patel, the motel manager and the person who'd made the 911 call, directed EMTs to room 231 on the second floor. The room appeared to be in the process of being cleaned. A pillow was on the bedside table. Bedcovers were placed on the desk. A red plastic bag with bottled water lay on the black-and-gold carpet near a desk chair. The room's iron, phone, microwave, TV, all seemed undisturbed.

Just beyond the bed, the bathroom door was slightly ajar, but nothing really seemed amiss. Certainly nothing to prepare EMTs Mark Easley and Shawn Ford for what they were about to find. Easley headed for the bathroom, but he was unable to enter because there was a body sprawled out on the floor. A halo of blood puddled around the victim's upper torso. Looking around the door, Easley was pretty sure the victim was dead. He dropped his aid bags, while medic Shawn Ford pushed past the half-cocked door into the bathroom.

The victim was laying catawampus with her head near the tub. Her legs were sprawled frog-like, her right knee almost touching the toilet. A massive amount of blood pooled underneath her head and her upper torso. A pair of eyeglasses were in the tub, near the faucet, a sign there had been some sort of struggle.

The young girl was dressed in a black lace tank top, a pair of jeans, and tennis shoes. Her clothes were all intact. A washcloth was balled up and lay near her mouth. Likely used to stifle any screams. Her eyes were wide open. Glaring at her murderer? A white shirt was bunched up underneath her, wrapped around her right arm. A green ink pen lay near her right shoulder, probably knocked out of her hands.

Ford squatted down beside the body, checked her left wrist for a pulse he was sure he wouldn't find. She was cold to the touch. Rigor had set in. He took note of the blood. There was blood on the victim's neck, across her breast region, a big puddle underneath her left shoulder flowing up to her left cheekbone. He scanned the room quickly, looking for a weapon. It was clear the victim had been stabbed, but there was no knife in sight.

The EMTs were waiting outside the room when Pendleton Police arrived a few moments later. Ford and Easley offered a brief rundown of what they'd found in the room, noting that the victim had been dead for some time. She was cold to the touch.

"Her top is low-cut, so I saw she has a large wound on her chest," Ford said.

"What kind of wound?" the officer asked.

"I can't say for sure, but it looks like it might be a stab wound."

"Any weapons?"

"I didn't see any," Ford said. "But I wasn't in there long. I checked her pulse and left."

"We didn't disturb anything," Easley added. "We've been waiting for you to get here. We did leave two medic bags with equipment near the bathroom door."

Once Sgt. Tony Nelson, the responding officer, knew he was dealing with a murder scene, he requested Lieutenant Bill Caldera and Detective Jim Littlefield be dispatched to the motel. Then he retrieved crime scene tape from his vehicle, along with his digital camera to photograph the scene.

Downstairs, Officer Paul Wolverton asked the Travelodge manager Kal Patel if he could use her office so he could speak in private with the motel's other housekeeper. The housekeeper noted that her English wasn't very good but she was able to communicate that she was the first person to find the dead girl, but she had no idea what had happened. She didn't know the new maid.

Afterward, Wolverton returned to room 231, where he found Sgt. Nelson briefing Detective Jim Littlefield and Lieutenant Bill Caldera outside the room. Nelson told them they didn't yet know who the victim was. Wolverton offered up a possible name given to him by the motel manager along with paperwork for an "Amanda King-Palmer." But they couldn't be sure if the girl on the floor was the Amanda associated with the paperwork. Wolverton said he'd check with Patel again to get a definite identification.

"See what else she knows, if anything, about this girl," Sgt. Nelson instructed.

While Wolverton dashed off to interview Kal Patel further, Detective Littlefield, Sgt. Nelson, and Lt. Caldera entered room 231 and began to photograph the crime scene. Walking around the bathroom door, Littlefield squatted down beside the murdered girl and performed a preliminary exam. He noted that the girl had been stabbed. He could see seven, maybe eight or more, puncture wounds. All the injuries were confined to a small area around the victim's breastplate, nearest her heart. Such violence was usually indicative of a crime of passion. An ex-boyfriend? A lover betrayed? Someone who knew the victim and was angry at her for some reason? Nelson videotaped as Littlefield did the exam. Before they were done with their task, Wolverton returned with a name for the victim: Amyjane Brandhagen.

Lt. Caldera wasn't sure he heard that right. *Amyjane?*

The Brandhagens and Calderas were longtime friends. Vicki Caldera and Dave Brandhagen had known each other since they were teenagers. When the newly married Calderas moved to Pendleton in 1987, Vicki introduced her husband to Dave and Cathy. Reserved by nature, Bill Caldera respected Dave Brandhagen's composed and calm manner. Both men possessed deep values rooted in a faith community, in sports, and in family. The couples got together for dinner out and the occasional social functions about town. Lt. Caldera knew Amyjane had recently gone on a mission trip. He could not imagine how it was she ended up in the pool of blood on the bathroom floor of the motel room. And he could not imagine anyone but him giving that news to her parents.

Someone asked if Lt. Caldera would be able to make a positive ID of the victim. Caldera had no idea how badly mutilated Amyjane's body might be. At that point, no one knew if Amyjane had been sexually assaulted or not. Whatever emotions Caldera had as a family friend to the Brandhagens were put aside: he was a professional officer with a job to do.

Caldera took a quick look into the bathroom at the bloodied body laying catawampus, a white shirt wrapped behind her and over her right arm, as if she had been using it as a cape, play-acting in death the way she did in daily life. There wasn't any doubt in his mind: this was Amyjane.[2]

Caldera was stricken by the violence of the scene. This was the first young adult murder of his law enforcement career. Stepping out of the bathroom, out of the shadows of room 231 and into the blinding light of a hot August afternoon, Caldera confirmed to Det. Jackson that yes, indeed, the dead girl was Amyjane Brandhagen.

"I'll make the notification to her parents," he added. "I know Dave and Cathy." Others knew them, too, but not the way Caldera did.

"All right," Det. Jackson said. "You sure?"

Caldera nodded. His mind was racing ahead. He needed to get ahold of his wife. He needed her at his side, but that meant giving her the news beforehand. Throughout their years together, Vicki was privy to many of his hardest moments as an officer. But nothing they'd ever been through before compared to this. Det. Jackson asked Sgt. Nelson to accompany Caldera.

"That trip across town was the longest of my life," Lt. Caldera recalled. In reality, the trip between the motel and the Brandhagen home was less than three miles. However, Caldera now recognizes that what made the trip so unbearable was his own state of shock and disbelief. He swung by Vicki's workplace and picked her up so that she could be there as a support for Cathy.

Silence filled the car as the couple made their way across town, along the tree-lined roads and past the split-level homes and the brightly dressed children at a nearby playground. Both Lt. Caldera and Vicki were lost in their own thoughts, remembering happier times shared with Dave and Cathy. Quiet tears fell as they thought of Amyjane, of the joy she had brought into the Brandhagens' home, the much longed-for child expanding their hearts, their home, and the community at large.

Sgt. Nelson, who had driven separately, met the Calderas outside the Brandhagens' house. They shared a brief exchange as they made the walk to the door. Caldera had not called ahead to see if Dave or Cathy were home. He feared doing so would result in the Brandhagens getting the news by phone, something a caring cop is loath to do but especially in this situation.

"I felt it was better to tell them in person," Caldera said.

So, when they knocked on the door, neither officer knew if anyone was home. If Cathy was the only one home, would they tell her first then wait for Dave to arrive? Or should she be the one to break the news to him? They hadn't ironed all that out before Dave, answering the knock, greeted them.

One look and Dave knew that whatever had brought these folks to his front door wasn't good news. He welcomed the Calderas and nodded at Sgt. Nelson. Lt. Caldera made the introductions and asked if Cathy was at home, too.

"Yes," Dave replied, stepping aside and inviting them all in.

"Vicki and I didn't normally visit them at their home, so Dave knew right way it wasn't good news," Lt. Caldera recalled. "Dave led Vicki and I and Tony (Sgt. Nelson) into the family room. Cathy joined us. I guess it was the family room. There was a pool table in the room. They offered me a seat, and they sat down as well. I told them I had some bad news for them. Of course, they'd already figured that out. I didn't see any need to draw it out, so I just said it: 'Amyjane was found beaten at the Travelodge. She's been murdered. It appears she was stabbed. We have the best detectives in the two-county area working the case.'"

Dave's head dropped to his chest. Cathy erupted into sobs, as did Lorabeth, Amyjane's younger sister, who was also present. "Cathy was in a definite state of shock," Caldera said. "I can't tell you how well Dave handled such tragic news. He was in shock, too, but he handled it well." By well, Caldera means that Dave didn't collapse in a heap on the floor, although had Dave done so, Caldera would have found that an entirely reasonable thing to do. What father ever expects to be told their child has been murdered?

The officers sat silent until there was a brief lull in the weeping. Then Caldera asked if Amyjane had problems with anyone that they knew of. Cathy said that Amyjane lived on her own in a downtown apartment. She added that Amyjane had a second job at Subway, but that was only a few hours a week.

Caldera asked if Amyjane had a boyfriend. Cathy said that Amyjane had recently broken up with a boy named Brandon, who worked at Wells Fargo. She added that the two had only gone out for a very short period. Cathy said she was with Amyjane the night before and nothing seemed amiss. Amyjane had said something about seeing someone by the name of Jake Thompson. Cathy thought that Jake might have been at Amyjane's apartment after she'd left, but she wasn't sure.

"Is there anyone else that she was hanging out with that you know of?" Caldera asked.

Amyjane's closest friend was Jacky Sheoships, Cathy reported. She didn't have an address for her. Oh. Yeah. And there was this new fellow—"Micah Smith, no, that's not right, Micah Parker"—that had been coming around, too. Amyjane had told her mom that Micah might have a thing for her. Micah lived in a yellow house at Olney Cemetery. His friends called him "the gatekeeper of the graveyard." Amyjane had told her mom that she was with Micah at McKay Dam a few days prior "to watch a meteor shower."

Lt. Caldera asked if Dave or Cathy could provide any information about their daughter's living situation. Cathy said the apartment complex was frequented or inhabited by some "shady people."

"Amyjane makes friends with everyone," Dave added. "She doesn't have any boundaries when speaking with others." It made her parents uneasy, this willingness on their daughter's behalf to befriend anyone. Like any good parents might, they constantly worried about Amyjane's safety.

"She usually left her apartment unlocked," Dave added.

Caldera asked if it would be all right for the police to enter her apartment to search it.

"Yes," Dave said. "Feel free."

Lorabeth said her sister had a laptop computer in her apartment. It was locked, but Lorabeth knew the passcode. There might be something on there that would help the police. She gave Caldera and Nelson the code: cog92love.

The one thing that Lt. Caldera didn't mention to Dave or Cathy, the one thing causing him personal consternation, was knowing that part of the investigation would require Dave and Cathy to be questioned and treated as "possible suspects."

"I knew in my heart that Dave and Cathy had nothing to do with it. I could never consider Dave and Cathy suspects," he said. But as a professional, Lt. Caldera knew that the investigation would have to run its course, which meant that Dave and Cathy would have to be treated as potential suspects. They would be interviewed.

They would be asked to provide DNA samples. He wouldn't do it, couldn't do it, but others in the department who didn't know the Brandhagens the way he knew them would look at the Brandhagens with the disturbing question of: could one of them have done this to their own daughter?

The bulk of all murders are committed by people we know and often love. Stranger murders are rare, averaging only about 11 percent.[3] The stab wounds Amyjane endured indicated a violence common among loved ones. The issue about who would question Dave and Cathy wasn't a decision for Lt. Caldera to make. His role was to be as much of a support to Dave and Cathy as he possibly could be during the forthcoming investigation. He reassured them of that as he was leaving. "You can call me anytime," Caldera said. "Day or night. I'm here for you." Then he and his wife drove away engulfed in mournful silence.

CHAPTER TWENTY-FIVE

With Chief Stuart Roberts out of town on vacation at the time, Detective Jackson put Detective Littlefield in charge of the investigation. Murders weren't a common occurrence in Umatilla County, but Littlefield had overseen his share of murder scenes over the course of his career. He knew the evidence police gathered in those first forty-eight hours would be critical to identifying the murderer.

Littlefield worked with Umatilla County's Major Crime team, an investigative team drawn from law enforcement agencies throughout the county who handled the region's homicides and suicides. There are cops in every agency who hate taking the dead body calls. Littlefield didn't especially love those calls, but they didn't unnerve him like they did some. Analytical by nature, he had taken advantage of extra learning opportunities for death investigation certification. Unlike Lt. Caldera and others on the force, Littlefield did not know the Brandhagen family. He approached the crime scene with experience and objectivity.

"It was clear from the beginning that this was a stabbing," Littlefield said. "There was no evidence of blunt force trauma. No gunshot wound. My initial thought was that she had been ambushed from behind. All the stab marks were centralized around the heart, in an area about the size of a compact disc."[1]

There was no sign of a struggle other than in the bathroom. Early on in his investigation, Det. Littlefield theorized that Amyjane likely never saw her killer before the attack. "The stab marks were perpendicular to her body. If she was standing up, I'd expect those wounds to be up and down in line with her body position, not perpendicular. My own theory is that her killer came up from behind her, grabbed her around the throat, choking her and taking her down to the ground."

Two adults in a struggle for life. Once Amyjane was on the floor, Littlefield imagined the killer crouched near her left side and continued stabbing her from that angle, thus creating the sideways wounds. "That bathroom was so small, it would be hard to get two people in there without great difficulty. The killer could have only been on her left side because there was no room on her right side," Littlefield said. "I don't believe he was in the bathroom before Amyjane entered because there was no sign of footwear in the shower. Most of the stabbing occurred on the floor of the bathroom."

Amyjane had to have been ambushed, Littlefield concluded. He could not determine for sure whether Amyjane knew her assailant or not, but the ferocity with which she was stabbed caused him to suspect that it was someone she knew. "A couple of the stab wounds went all the way through Amyjane," Littlefield said. "Whoever killed her did so with a great deal of force. There were poke marks in the linoleum underneath her. For that kind of force, you must have pretty good leverage. It could be that as her killer choked her, Amyjane hit her head on the tub on the way down and was knocked unconscious. So she may have been unable to fight back."

That kind of viciousness is usually indicative of strong emotion—anger. Whoever killed Amyjane Brandhagen was one very angry, angry person, Littlefield deduced. A lover spurned, perhaps? "This was a very emotional kind of crime. Whoever did this seemed to have a heartfelt connection with the victim. Someone she had a relationship with, maybe? I did wonder if she had a relationship with somebody and broke their heart, and now, they were breaking hers."

Unanswered questions dog every detective. The one that would keep Littlefield awake throughout the coming year was what had made Amyjane's killer so very angry.

CHAPTER TWENTY-SIX

nvestigators began the tedious process of documenting evidence retrieved from the crime scene: Amyjane's purse containing her cell phone, a fan, tissue, and an appointment card for Umatilla County Public Health Clinic dated August 20th. They carefully removed hair strands and nail clippings. All these things were bagged and logged as the first pieces of evidence in the case. The fingernail clippings and hair strands would be sent off to the Oregon State Forensic Crime Lab for processing. Amyjane's phone was taken to the Pendleton Police Station where its contents were downloaded.

The motel maid who discovered Amyjane was interviewed again, this time by a Spanish-speaking detective, who recorded the conversation. A twenty-three-year employee of the motel, the housekeeper said that she barely knew Amyjane, but she had seen her that morning around eleven thirty. They did not speak to one another. She did not see Amyjane again for the rest of the day until she entered that room after the manager instructed her to find the new hire. She had thought that perhaps Amyjane had walked off the job. The one thing she had found strange prior to discovering the dead girl was that the doors to the other rooms assigned to Amyjane were all open.

Normally, housekeepers kept the doors locked until they were ready to clean them. Why did Amyjane have all the doors open?

City Hall is directly across from the motel. A parking lot and a one-way street separate the two facilities. Investigators were hopeful that they might retrieve some clues from video surveillance cameras at the motel and from City Hall, but Kal Patel informed them that the video in the motel's lobby wasn't working. There was no video available from the Travelodge.

Several officers searched the river levee, which was located north of the motel. They checked garbage cans, looking for a murder weapon, anything that might provide further evidence. They interviewed people who were near the Travelodge. Neighbors. Passersby. And a motel handyman, who had been painting in several of the rooms that day. Officer Wolverton requested a list of all the occupants of the motel during the two days prior and including the day the body was discovered.

Pendleton Police and the Umatilla County Major Crime team did their due diligence during those early crucial hours following the murder. No possibility was ruled out. Not initially, at least.

CHAPTER TWENTY-SEVEN

W hen Amyjane left her apartment for work that Tuesday morning, she had no idea that she would not be returning at the end of that workday. So, when Pendleton police entered her apartment, they found it just as she had left it—a hot mess. Clothes were strewn about; books, journals, cards were piled up on a desk. Her bed was unmade. Yet there was no sign of a struggle of any sort. No sign that anyone had ransacked her apartment.

They found a pair of panties on the bathroom floor with bloodstains in the crotch and a tampon container in the trash can nearby. A green bath towel with what appeared to be bloodstains was found in her bed. Police seized these items—the panties and the bath towel—along with several other items. All the sheets, pillowcases, and bedcoverings; two packages of condoms, one from the trash can in the bathroom, and one laying on the floor next to the trash can; several notebooks with journal writing, poetry, and drawings; various envelopes, one labeled "Chancy letters," one labeled "Chancy Poems," and one labeled "Donald." All these items were placed in the evidence locker at the police station.

Chancy Yates was just one of several young men that Amyjane

was romantically linked to. A popular and vivacious girl, kind and big-hearted, Amyjane collected boyfriends the way some people collect travel trinkets. Her charisma and charm drew people in. Her warmth and nurturing ways held them in her spell. Amyjane was perceived by most about town as a "good Christian girl." She was that and more. She was actively involved in many different church activities and outreaches. She had studied and served with the national organization Youth With A Mission (YWAM). Her faith was deep. Her desire to please God unquestionable. Yet Amyjane did not embrace the celibate lifestyle expected of young girls brought up in Evangelical households. Promise rings and father-daughter banquets aside, Amyjane was a woman of many passions. Those who knew her primarily through religious affiliations or by association with her parents were surprised when investigators began to question them about her sexual activity.

Amyjane's active sex life would complicate the investigation in a myriad of ways. The public at large simply had no clue about how many leads the police would have to chase down. Investigators didn't have a clue how many males they would have to pursue to submit to DNA testing. So, when police first discovered a "Depo shot" notation for August 20th on a calendar in Amyjane's kitchen, they didn't give it much thought; still they took the calendar into evidence.

It was past six p.m. when Officer Wolverton and his partner arrived back at the Brandhagens' home to conduct more formal interviews with Amyjane's parents and sister. Only a few hours had passed since Lt. Caldera first informed the family of Amyjane's murder, but police had a killer to find. The officers began by interviewing and recording Cathy alone. This is standard operating procedure for any crime, whether it's a juvenile offense or a murder. Professional cops conduct interviews by separating potential offenders and interviewing them individually. Cathy was forthcoming, repeating some of the very same information she had provided earlier.

Amyjane, her mom said, was a sweet, joyful girl who loved the Lord but who "hangs on the edge." Asked to clarify what she meant by that, Cathy explained that one of her daughter's favorite things to do was to contact and talk to strangers. This habit concerned her family greatly. While they loved her open nature, they feared for her safety.

Cathy gave Officer Wolverton some of the names of Amyjane's friends and some of the young men that she was romantically linked to. She'd dated Chancy Yates briefly after she'd returned from a YWAM trip in April. Cathy noted that the two had only been an item for a little over a month but that Chancy had recently told her that he was still in love with Amyjane and that he would always love her. Amyjane moved out of her parents' home in May and had begun seeing a fellow by the name of Brandon, but that relationship had come to a halt by mid-July.

Most recently, Amyjane had been hanging out with two brothers: Adam and Micah Parker. The trio had met when Amyjane began attending Pendleton's Foursquare Church. Cathy said that when she was with her daughter the previous night, Amyjane said, "I think Micah has a cute little crush on me." Cathy threw out some more names that she thought might be helpful to the investigation, including a tidbit about a former coworker of her daughter's that Cathy was suspicious of. She described him as a dark-haired fella with a penchant for dressing goth, with spikey wristbands and dark clothing.

The interviews with Dave and Lorabeth weren't nearly as detailed or as forthcoming. Dave said he would occasionally meet his daughter for coffee and a casual visit, but when it came to her personal life, who she had dated or was dating, what friend she may have had a falling out with, who her coworkers were, Cathy knew that sort of information. Dave added that Amyjane was a sweet girl who rooted for the underdog and would do anything to keep the peace with others. She was not confrontational in nature. He couldn't think of any enemies she had made or why anyone would want to murder his daughter.

Lorabeth had even less to divulge. She and Amyjane respected each other's privacy. They were not the kind of sisters who shared every intimate detail of their lives. Lorabeth could identify some of the people who lived in the same apartment complex as Amyjane, but she really had nothing to add as to who her sister might have been seeing or who might have a reason to want to see her sister dead. Lorabeth said Amyjane would mostly talk to their mom about her romantic endeavors, not her.

By the time Wolverton and his partner left the Brandhagen home that evening, they had a working list of names of those within Amyjane's inner circle. They had no idea how quickly or how wide that circle would expand. Or how exhausting the hunt for Amyjane's killer would become.

CHAPTER TWENTY-EIGHT

Investigators began tracking down the ever-growing list of Amyjane's boyfriends, current and former and the wannabes, as well as her friends, coworkers, and acquaintances, interviewing everyone, asking them all the same questions: What was their relationship to the victim? Where were they on Tuesday, August 14th? And who could corroborate their whereabouts?

Micah Parker, who had that little crush on Amyjane, didn't have any trouble identifying his whereabouts. He'd been at the Oregon coast, a good six or more–hour drive away with his brother and some friends. Chancy Yates, the fellow whose notes to Amyjane were found by police in an envelope on her desk, had spent the day moving into a new apartment, with the help of his sister and his new girlfriend. Only one of the young men interviewed offered up conflicting stories of his whereabouts for the previous day. That fellow was Sullivan Jim. Police were familiar with Sullivan Jim before Cathy Brandhagen identified him as a troublesome person in Amyjane's life. The two had dated off and on throughout their high school years, much to Cathy's chagrin.[1]

As a member of the Confederated Tribes of the Umatilla Indians, Sullivan Jim lived on the reservation at Mission, just outside of Pendleton. He was a familiar person of interest to police. "We narrowed the investigation to Sullivan Jim pretty quickly," Detective Littlefield recalled. Within the first forty-eight hours, actually.

"Sullivan was known to be a drinker and a pretty volatile guy," Littlefield said. "Witnesses said that the two had had an argument in the days before Amyjane was murdered. He wanted to get back with her, but Amyjane didn't want to." The two were in almost obsessive contact with one another. Cell phone records indicated that from July 7th to July 28th, there were 316 calls or text messages exchanged between the couple.

It didn't help matters that Sullivan Jim was less than forthcoming when investigators initially reached out to him. When police arrived at his home, Jim's sister told police that her brother was not at home. A few hours later, Jim called police and said on the day of the murder he'd been at the Reservation where he'd visited Mission Market and Wildhorse Casino. Later, perhaps realizing that police could verify his story through video cameras, he told police he had made up that story. He was at home the day of the murder, and he had even been at home when the police had stopped by after Amyjane's death.

Police questioned why he hadn't told the truth. Jim said that there was an arrest warrant out for him on other unrelated charges, and he didn't want to go to jail. He also said he wanted to protect his sister, who had lied to police on his behalf. Jim said it was true that he and Amyjane were an item during their high school years and that they had remained friends since. He added that the last time he'd seen her was about two weeks prior when he'd spent the night at her apartment. Jim agreed to come to the police station the next day to sit for a formal interview.

Sullivan Jim's profile as the possible killer had escalated in investigators' minds after the handyman at the Travelodge told police he had seen a man matching Jim's height and coloring lurking around the motel early on the day of the murder. The handyman noticed a man he described as either "Hispanic" or "Native American" walking from the back parking lot through the motel's breezeway to the front of the building. He saw him twice that day. The last time he saw him was around noon. He added that he'd finished work around one thirty p.m. so he had to have seen the fella before that. Yet, when police showed him a photo of Sullivan Jim and said that Amyjane had been in a relationship with him, the handyman was still unable to identify for certain that Jim was the young man he'd seen the day of the murder. "The hair isn't right," he said. "The man I saw had bushier hair."

Investigators pressed him for more details. The handyman said that the young man he saw was wearing brown corduroy slacks and had a thin mustache; otherwise, he was clean cut. A few days later, the handyman told police he'd seen the young man again. This time, he was walking toward the river levee, a popular walking and running path along the Umatilla River that flows through the heart of the city. Despite that new information, police kept their focus on Amyjane's ex. "Based on the information we had at that time, Sullivan Jim became a very likely suspect," Det. Littlefield said.

While Sullivan Jim became a "very likely suspect" in the murder, he wasn't the only one. A girlfriend of Amyjane's told police that the murdered girl was in a relationship with a married man out of Tacoma, Washington. The two had met in an online chat room, and he'd driven down to Pendleton a couple of times to hook up with her. This alarmed police. This fellow was a completely unknown entity. A married man who was having a relationship of somewhat questionable nature with the victim. If he was sexually involved with the victim, was this an act of revenge? Had his wife found out? Had he and Amyjane had some sort of violent encounter? Who was this man? And what exactly was the nature of his relationship with the victim? Police were able to extract a name from the victim's friend, but that's about all they had to go on.

FBI Special Agent Alex White was tasked with tracking down the Tacoma suspect and bringing the man in for an interview regarding the nature of his relationship with Amyjane. The sheer list of potential suspects in this murder case seemed to be growing by the minute. The amount of manpower and hours it would take to track down all the people Amyjane was involved with was formidable.

CHAPTER TWENTY-NINE

Amyjane was a writer who wrote poetry and short stories. She journaled. She experimented with science fiction and magical realism. She was a thinker, an explorer, an adventurer, both in her writings and in her life. Like a lot of young adults, she processed her emotions into creative energy. Commenting on the social media site Tumblr in 2011 about a particularly difficult time in her life, Amyjane noted, "Parents are just hurt kids who had kids. They really do love you with all their heart. It just gets filtered through their past and pain." Her writings often give insight into her relationships with others, her place in the world, and her thoughts about her worth: "Deep within myself, I used to believe the wrong person was born, the wrong one made it. That I was a mistake, even if I was wanted."

Many of her entries are addressed to God in a diary-like format. They are very personal and filled with the tension of a young girl conflicted because her actions were too often at odds with the person she wanted to be, or perhaps with the person her parents and others wanted her to be. Shortly before she was murdered, Amyjane posted a note about a new word she had learned—Athazagoraphobia, the fear of being ignored, forgotten, or replaced. "I didn't know this was a real phobia," she wrote. "And guess what? If I am honest, I have it." She could never have imagined how her death would ensure that her short life would never be forgotten.

Photos of Amyjane on her mission trip to India show her surrounded by children. They laughed with her, danced with her, climbed upon her limbs, and sat in her arm crooks as if she were an ancient oak to be explored. Shortly after her return from mission work in India, Amyjane wrote these prescient words: "Lord, why can't I just stay with you? Why do I have to live in this world? All I want is you. I hate having to fight every day."

If he had kept a diary, those are words Luke might have penned himself. He, too, had gone on mission trips, had prayed to the same God, had wondered about his place in the world and the meaning to his life, and planned for his future. He had hopes and dreams and was every bit as passionate about them as Amyjane.

Autopsies are handled by the state medical examiner's office. Amyjane's was scheduled for Thursday, August 16, 2012, in Clackamas, Oregon, about a three-hour drive west of Pendleton. Two detectives— Brandon Gomez of Pendleton Police and Leonard Stokoe of the county's Major Crimes Team Task Force—were in attendance.

Dr. Christopher Young conducted Amy's autopsy.[1] The process isn't a quick one. Dissecting and recording abrasions, wounds, both remarkable and unremarkable, collecting tissue samples, and collecting anything at all that might lead to the all-important DNA link to the killer is a tedious process. Young took his time, aware of how important the slightest loose hair or light bruise could be. His findings were detailed in a multi-page report: <u>Cause of death:</u> Homicidal Violence Including Multiple Stab Wounds and Strangulation. <u>Manner of death:</u> Homicide.

Investigators had wrapped her hands in bags and those bags were sealed with tape, a way to protect any DNA evidence. Dr. Young was able to extract several loose hairs found on the front of Amyjane's top and her pants. She was found fully clothed. He noted that she wore her class ring marked "Amyjane" and "PHS 2011." In typical Amyjane fashion, she was wearing one navy sock and one pink-striped sock.

There were injuries to her eyes and blood in her nasal cavities, although there were no injuries to her mouth or lips. The hemorrhaging in her eyes was the result of strangulation. There were no defensive wounds on either hand, indicating that Amyjane did not fight her attacker. There was some hemorrhaging under the scalp, mostly on the left side of her head. It is this injury that might explain why Amyjane couldn't fight back. She appeared to have taken a blow to the head.

Dr. Young determined that Amyjane had suffered multiple stab wounds, eight to be exact, three directly to the heart. The penetration of the stab wounds was five to six inches, likely the length of the blade used. There was a perforation of Amy's sternum, her left lung, aorta, and esophagus, all with a front-to-back trajectory.

The doctor also made notes about a tattoo found on Amyjane's upper right back. It was two interlocking crescent moons. One was solid ink and decorated with stars. The other simply contained a reference to Psalms 139, a hymn of praise, whose most oft-quoted verses are: "For you created my inmost being, you knit me together in my mother's womb. I praise you because I am fearfully and wonderfully made." For a child who is adopted, these verses can be a solace, a reminder that despite the circumstances that led to their birth mother putting them up for adoption, they have value and are worthy before God and man. But Psalms 139 contains other verses that certainly would have escaped the attention of a bright and optimistic gal like Amyjane. Verses that seem eerily prophetic in retrospect: "If only you, God, would slay the wicked. Away from me, you who are bloodthirsty."

It would take several weeks for all the lab work from the autopsy to be completed, but the final report was telling. The report revealed Amyjane had quantities of methamphetamine, amphetamine, morphine, and an anti-depressant drug in her system. According to Oregon State Police Forensics, the level of meth in Amy's system indicated that she had ingested the drug sometime within forty-eight hours prior to her death. This finding surprised those in law enforcement who knew the Brandhagen family, and especially those who knew Amyjane. These findings, especially the discovery of meth, meant that police would have to widen their investigation to include an even broader range of potential suspects.

CHAPTER THIRTY

While Amyjane's autopsy was taking place, Sullivan Jim was meeting with investigators at the Oregon State Police offices in Pendleton. Jim had no idea he was the primary suspect in Amyjane's murder, but he understood that he was in trouble for lying to police about his whereabouts on the afternoon Amyjane was killed. So he willingly agreed to meet with investigators.

Prior to the interview, police had collected a note from Amyjane's apartment. The double-sided note read, "Gone to work, you can let yourself out. Milk in the fridge." It was signed by Amyjane. On the flip side was a response from Jim: "Thanks, it was nice seeing you again. It was nice to hear your voice and laughter once more." They asked Jim about the note. He said a couple of weeks earlier he was outside Crabby's Saloon, a local pub, when he ran into Amyjane. Jim said he'd been drinking and was intoxicated at the time. He and Amyjane struck up a conversation and eventually ended up at her apartment. Jim denied that the two had been intimate that night. Instead, he said, they had stayed up most of the night just talking, until they both finally fell asleep. He said when he woke up, Amyjane was gone. Her note was on the table. "That was the last time I saw or talked to her," he said.

Investigators weren't sure they believed him. Several of Amyjane's friends had already been interviewed by officers. Those friends had said that Jim had a temper. They'd given officers examples of when they'd seen Sullivan Jim lose his composure. One friend said he had acted violently toward Amyjane when the two were dating. Pressed to give details, this friend said that they had never actually witnessed Jim strike her but that Amyjane had told them about a time when Jim had punched a locker near her head. All of this was hearsay, the sort of gossip that happens in the aftermath of a crime, and the small-town atmosphere of Pendleton had long made gossip a favorite community pastime.

Gossip could be a double-edged sword for investigators. People were willing to talk, to share their insights, but they weren't always sticklers for factual details, and criminal cases are built upon facts. Still, investigators had to follow up every lead sent their way, even the rumor that Jim and Amyjane had had an argument the weekend before her death, a rumor that Jim vehemently denied. He stuck with his story that he hadn't seen Amyjane since the night he was at her apartment. Yet investigators could hardly take him at his word, given that he had already lied to them. He certainly seemed like somebody with something to hide.

Would he be willing to submit to a polygraph?

"Yes," Jim replied, much to the investigator's surprise.

Throughout the polygraph, Jim was nervous. He fidgeted. He tapped his feet. His breathing grew heavy and labored at times, as if he were running a race. Even his heart rate was elevated. All these behaviors were especially pronounced when the officer administering the test asked Jim if he was at the Travelodge when Amyjane was killed.

"No," he replied.

When asked if he had killed Amyjane, Jim was adamant that he had nothing to do with her murder. He said he wasn't even in Pendleton at the time. When the investigator asked why he was seemingly so anxious—the foot tapping, the labored breathing—Jim said it was because of how much he cared for Amyjane. He was upset over her murder.

Loving another person doesn't preclude that you might also want to kill them. Jealous, murderous rages have put more than one person behind bars. Police were told that Jim was the jealous sort. He had reportedly approached one of Amy's friends and tried to enlist her help in hooking the two back up. The friend declined, repeating the thing Amy had been trying to tell him for some time—she just wanted to be friends with him.

What he didn't know, what few people knew, was just how many romantic entanglements Amyjane had going on. Investigators had the job now of trying to unravel all those entanglements to determine who had reason enough to murder Amyjane in such a violent manner. It was a momentous task, complicated by the fact that the crime scene itself provided them with so little evidence. Someone had walked into room 231, directly across the street from City Hall, and murdered a girl in broad daylight. Then seemingly vanished into thin air.

To the surprise of many, including investigators, Jim passed the lie detector test. Then he voluntarily submitted to a saliva test for DNA comparison. Furthermore, he agreed that investigators could photograph his body, his clothes, and his shoes. If Sullivan Jim was a guilty man, he sure wasn't acting like one.

Nonetheless, given all the rumors on the street about who Sullivan Jim was and the nature of his relationship with Amyjane, there were cops who, despite the results of the lie detector test, despite Jim's willingness to submit to DNA testing, and despite his cooperation with police, believed wholeheartedly that Sullivan Jim had killed Amyjane Brandhagen. One cannot rule out the possibility that inherent bias played into those assumptions. Pendleton is no more immune from the racism that runs rampant in this country than any other community. Racist remarks about Tribal people are not uncommon among the town's primarily white populace.

"A lot of times, police think they know what happened," Det. Littlefield explained. "Once they make up their minds, it's hard to get them off that because they are so sure they know. Cops are supposed to know everything. I kept urging them to bring me the hardest piece of evidence they had—video, fingerprints, DNA, anything. You must let the evidence lead you. Rumor is not hard evidence. You have to follow the evidence." Despite increasing frustration among investigators and the fearful community at large who were pressing police for an arrest, this would become the Pendleton Police Department's mantra for the murder investigation: *follow the evidence.*

If not Sullivan Jim, who then? Who had done this evil thing? Why? Why had they done this horrible thing? Where were they now? And were others at risk? Cops needed to make an arrest before the killer answered that last question for them.

CHAPTER THIRTY-ONE

The local paper reported what sketchy details they had about the murder as they continued to press Chief Roberts for more information. In frustration, editors at the newspaper took to Facebook and posted this message: "For those of you wondering, law enforcement has not provided any updates to the *East Oregonian* on the Amyjane Brandhagen homicide. If you have any information that could help, call Pendleton Police."

Funeral services for Amyjane were set for Tuesday, August 21st, at ten a.m., at the Free Methodist Church in Pendleton. Amyjane was a member of the Free Methodist Church. She started out in the church nursery and was there in 2011 when the congregation recognized their graduating seniors. She played puzzles and made her first friends in the church's preschool class. She drew an ark with animals in Vacation Bible School and learned to memorize and recite John 3:16—"For God so loved the world, He gave his only begotten son . . . " She wore itchy lace socks and dresses for Easter services. She learned the words to "Amazing Grace" and "I Can Only Imagine" and learned to lose herself in worship of Jesus Christ, her Lord and Savior.

Amyjane was as much at home in church as she was anyplace else in the world. People at church called her by name. They prayed for her and over her. They hugged her every coming and going. Within the doors of the church, Amyjane learned the truest lessons of life: Be kind to all you meet because you entertain angels unaware. Walk humbly. Love God. Love others. Love mercy. Do all the good you can all the ways you can for as long as you can.

It was only right that one long week after her murder, and just days after her autopsy, Amyjane Brandhagen was memorialized by her very loving and brokenhearted church family. They swapped stories and shared Kleenexes and tender hugs. They cried and laughed over their most treasured memories of Amyjane. They sang songs and imagined her dancing at the throne of God. How she loved to dance! Mostly, they grieved together, which is how all grief is best endured, within a community of people who have loved you deeply. Amyjane had loved deeply, and in return she was deeply loved.

Friends and loved ones planned a candlelight vigil for that same evening at Pendleton's Roy Raley Park, one of the places that held fond memories for Amyjane. Community members were encouraged to bring their own candles. Some brought sidewalk chalk and created memorials of bright pinks and yellows and blues in honor of the artist, poet, and creative that defined Amyjane. A couple of hundred mourners turned out. People of all ages. Many who knew Amyjane personally and many who didn't know her at all but were grieving that something so horrible could have happened here in this cowboy town they loved so well.

A thunderstorm, a rarity in the area, kicked off the morning. Amyjane loved thunderstorms. She once wrote that the best way to shower was to dance barefoot in the rain. That evening, as people gathered at the park and swapped their favorite memories of the beloved and joyful girl stolen from them, a warm summer wind blew in, blowing out some of the candles, forcing attendees to cup the golden light, protecting it from the falling darkness.

Local law enforcement attended the vigil. Those who knew the Brandhagen family wondered how in the world they could cope had it been one of their own children instead. Many vowed silently to do everything in their power to find Amyjane's killer and bring justice to the grieving family. Investigators who didn't know Amyjane beforehand came to know her through the tears and laughter and stories of those who loved her best. As they listened to the speakers, they searched the crowd carefully, looking upon each person with a raised eyebrow, a heightened sense of awareness. Wondering as different people proclaimed their love for Amy—could they be her killer?

He was there. The killer. In the shadows, listening to the stories and songs, watching a community and a family grieve. Thinking about the life he took, feeling extremely powerful at the way he had brought a community and a people to their knees. His chest swelled with a misbegotten pride over his evil deed. The tears of others brought a smile to his face. Dominion over others is an intoxicating drug. Once ingested, it becomes a craving. In the darkness, he slipped off toward the river, completely unnoticed, which was how he had spent the bulk of his life.

CHAPTER THIRTY-TWO

Two days after the funeral, FBI tracked down the married man in Tacoma, Washington, who reportedly had been in a relationship with Amyjane. FBI agent Todd Bakken interviewed both Calen Tackett and his wife.[1] When asked where they were on the day of Amyjane's murder, Calen said that he and his wife were at the dentist most of the morning. Afterward, Calen said that he visited a guitar shop while his wife shopped at a clothing store nearby. Then they stopped by the bank before heading home, where they spent the rest of the day. Calen confessed that he had met Amyjane twice in Pendleton. He said they had met online about three years earlier, in a chat room for poets and musicians. He knew her as "Amana," her online persona.

Calen said the two met face-to-face for the first time in September 2011, when he drove from Tacoma to Pendleton. They met at Roy Raley Park, the same park where the candlelight vigil took place. He said they met there because she was still living at home and didn't have her own apartment. During their time at the park, Calen said the two engaged in sex. He hung around for about five hours before driving back to Tacoma. For her part, Amyjane makes no mention of their meeting. However, in the days beforehand, she posted this tidbit of advice: "Gents, don't ask her out, just take her out. It usually ends better." In mid-September, she left Pendleton for her YWAM training.

The guitar player's second trip to Pendleton occurred in July 2012, about a month before her murder. They met up again at the same park, went to lunch, and eventually made their way back to Amyjane's apartment. They visited with some of her neighbors, then watched a movie together. He spent the night but insisted that they did not engage in sex. He said he left early the next morning, around five thirty a.m., and had not seen Amyjane since. When asked by the FBI agent if he would provide his DNA for testing, Calen agreed. The FBI requested no such DNA sample from his wife, however, because the agent felt like she had been forthcoming in her interview, confirming the timeline Calen had given regarding their whereabouts on the day of Amyjane's murder.

As Calen was being interviewed by the FBI, Chief Roberts sat down with reporter Phil Wright of the *East Oregonian*. Roberts hoped to quell the rumors snaking their way through the wheat fields and coffee shops and taverns about town. He told the reporter that there were eight to twelve detectives working the case, interviewing potential suspects, reviewing video footage collected from local businesses, sharing information with one another. He declined again to identify the way Amyjane was killed. "Roberts said Brandhagen did not suffer dozens of stab wounds, as one rumor indicated," Wright reported. Technically true. It wasn't dozens of stab wounds, but somewhat misleading, which likely was the chief's intent, to keep details of the murder out of the press, to protect the integrity of the case.

Roberts did confirm that the forensic report had been completed, but neither he nor Dan Primus, Umatilla County's district attorney, were willing to release the autopsy report or comment on the crime scene. "Keeping critical details of the case from the public makes it easier for police to sift through suspects and witness statements. This case is particularly tough, Roberts said, because police don't have a suspect," Wright added.

That much was true. Police didn't have one suspect. They had a growing list of suspects, and yet Roberts still questioned whether he was dealing with a serial killer. There were just so many possibilities. So many unanswered questions. So many DNA samples to collect and compare. "Roberts said he can't tell citizens if there is or isn't a killer on the loose in town," Wright reported. "Police just don't have enough information to say, and until otherwise advised, people need to stay diligent, let others know when and where you go and don't go around alone."

CHAPTER THIRTY-THREE

Nearly a year passed, and Pendleton police still had not made any arrests in the case. There was talk about town about the unsolved murder, but it didn't dominate coffee table talk like it had those first few months. Whenever the subject did come up it was often in the form of criticism that the murderer had gotten away with it. For most, the initial fear of the slaying had subsided, and locals had returned to their regular routines, but for the Brandhagens and the Pendleton police, Amyjane's murder was still a daily reality. The anniversary of her death was pressing in, and with it a sense of frustration for investigators, and for Chief Roberts a nagging sense of dread. He was keenly aware that anniversaries can hold significance for serial killers. A time when they might feel the need to strike again, to seek that high killing gives them.

The call of a missing fifty-three-year-old woman came into Pendleton dispatch at 11:08 p.m. on Friday, August 9, 2013, almost a year to the day of Amyjane's murder.[1] Dan Lange said his wife, Karen, had gone for a walk around the river levee earlier and failed to return. She'd left around five thirty p.m., a time of the day when the blazing Eastern Oregon sun begins to cool just a little. The high that Friday was ninety-five degrees. It was eighty-six degrees when Karen headed out. Sunset wasn't scheduled until nearly eight thirty. She had plenty of time to walk the levee and still make it home before dark. Walking the path around the Umatilla River was something Karen did on a regular basis, but by ten p.m., when she still wasn't home, Dan began to worry. Karen was almost always home before dark. He called her cell phone numerous times, but when those calls went unanswered, Dan went in search of her. He found her car parked in front of a friend's house on Northwest Tenth Street, the same place she usually parked. A group of friends and family joined Dan in the search.

Darkness settled over the river. The waning crescent moonlight cast dark shadows over the brush bordering the river as friends and loved ones searched. They walked the levee in tandem, calling out Karen's name, believing that some medical emergency had occurred and caused her to be unable to respond or get herself help. They took turns calling her cell phone, but she never answered. When they happened upon a Pendleton police officer, they alerted him that a woman was missing. With his assistance, they filed a missing person's report. With midnight growing nigh and still no sign of her, Dan grew increasingly distraught.

The community knew Amyjane Brandhagen's killer was "out there" somewhere. In their frustration, disgruntled folks referred to the Pendleton police force as "the Keystone Cops." Some suggested they would have to wait for "a deathbed confession" before a killer would ever be named. For the most part, the community simply had no idea how hard law enforcement was working the case. As Dan and others looked for Karen that night, the fear that the killer may have resurfaced near the anniversary of Amyjane's death nagged at them, prompting some to pray as they searched. Finally, in the wee morning darkness, exhausted and fearful, the search party dispersed back to their own homes to await daybreak when they could resume their efforts.

Shortly before seven a.m. the next morning, Detective Brandon Gomez discovered a body in heavy brush about thirty feet off the path in a secluded area behind the Bob White baseball field. "I found her lying on her back with her hands resting on her chest and her fingers interlocked," Gomez recalled. "Her head was soaked in blood from a gaping wound on the right side. Her face was covered in dried blood, as were her hands. Both of her eyes were extremely bruised and completely shut. Large amounts of blood were on the ground around her body. I did not receive a response when I called out her name, nor did I see any movement. She was laying there so motionless, I initially believed her to be dead." He called dispatch and told them to send help.

As he knelt over the body, Gomez noticed someone walking toward them. He left Karen and yelled at the pedestrian to go back the way he came. He didn't need any looky-sees compromising the crime scene. Then he returned to the victim and knelt to check her pulse. Karen flinched slightly. Her movement startled the detective. Inching closer, Gomez saw a slight rise in her chest. He called dispatch again and told them to get medics there ASAP. Turning his attention back to Karen, Gomez said, "Hang in there. Help is on the way. I'm here. You're safe now." Words of comfort and reassurance from a cop who was doing his best. "I wanted her to know that help was there now."

By the time medics arrived, Karen Lange had spent over thirteen hours mostly unconscious, slowly bleeding nearly to death in the thickets along the Umatilla River. Chief Roberts suspected almost immediately that whoever had done this thing to Karen Lange had also likely been the killer of Amyjane Brandhagen. It was too close to the anniversary of Amyjane's murder. It was just the sort of signature thing a serial killer would do.

As staff at St. Anthony's Hospital rushed into action to try and save Karen's life, Pendleton police sealed off the crime scene. The urgency to find the killer that they had felt in the immediate aftermath of Amyjane's death had grown a bit latent. Police were bogged down with dozens of false starts and outright lies. It was wearisome trying to wade through all the finger-pointing. But the discovery of Karen

Lange reawakened that earlier fervor. Police knew they needed to identify the killer, or another victim would soon fall prey.

That Dan and Karen Lange attended the very same church as Dave and Cathy Brandhagen was lost on no one. Both families were beloved members of Pendleton's Free Methodist Church. Karen was the worship leader at the church. Dan, who taught music at Blue Mountain Community College, also pitched in to help with worship at the church. Was someone specifically targeting women at the church? Was that the link that promted the killer to single out these two women? And who might the killer attack next? Those were the questions pressing in on investigators.

Saturday mornings at the levee are busy with joggers and walkers, kids headed to ballgames and the skate park. Police secured the crime scene, rerouting moms pushing strollers, kids on skateboards, dads carrying kids, and kids carrying gloves. One jogger told police about an older man he saw jump over a wall from behind the Pendleton rodeo grounds. He saw that the man's hands were bloodied. He called out and asked if the fella was okay, but the man headed off toward the river. He thought maybe the fellow was drunk or high. The officer took the passerby's information and recorded the information he provided.

A quick search in the area where Karen was found turned up the weapon her attacker likely used. Det. Gomez eyed a loose piece of plywood leaning up against a storage building near the baseball field, the perfect spot for someone looking to get rid of something in a hurry. Tilting the plywood so that the sunlight would expose anything behind it, Gomez saw a piece of galvanized pipe on the ground. There appeared to be dried blood on one end of the pipe. The pipe was photographed and removed for further examination and possible DNA.

Police had already obtained the DNA profiles of over fifty people associated with Amyjane, including five guests at the Travelodge; numerous known sex offenders; her closest friends; Calen, the married man from Tacoma; Sullivan Jim; a handful of local criminals;

and one mentally disturbed man who found Amyjane's number and began texting her after her death. They even ran a DNA profile on Dave Brandhagen and a cousin of Cathy's. The cousin was a Vietnam veteran who suffered from PTSD and admittedly annoyed Cathy because he said Cathy was far more serious by nature than him. This is the sort of thing that happens when there is no obvious killer and the case drags on and on. Detectives ended up chasing rumors down rabbitholes that have more twists and turns than Washington state's Rattlesnake Ridge.

One informant told police that he knew the two men involved in the killing of Amyjane. He claimed one of them witnessed the other one "gutting her" and that afterward the men had thrown their bloodied clothes and the knife used to kill Amyjane into the Umatilla River. This report was initially not considered reliable since Amyjane wasn't killed in the manner the informant described. But then, the girlfriend of one of the men told police that she believed her boyfriend had indeed killed Amyjane. This informant said her boyfriend regularly talked about killing people and had even claimed to have buried a body outside of Pendleton. She discovered a notebook he kept in which he wrote that he liked to choke, strangle, stab, and rape people. Of course, at that point, police perked up. Perhaps this informant was on to something.

She went on to explain that her boyfriend liked to choke her during intercourse, and for that reason and because of the things he'd written in his notebook, she believed he had murdered Amyjane. When police asked if there was any reference to Amyjane in the notebook, she said no. But her boyfriend was a known meth user and sometimes dealer. The toxicology report showed that Amyjane had ingested meth sometime in the forty-eight hours prior to her death, so investigators were rightly suspicious. They didn't know how Amyjane had obtained the meth. Every tip that came into the station had to be thoroughly vetted. It wasn't outside the realm of possibility that this known drug-user keeping a diary of his deepest, most troubling desires may have killed Amyjane. Detectives were obligated to chase down every potential suspect, and they had spent hours, days, months, a year doing just that. False leads can demand as much attention as viable leads, initially.

Chief Roberts told his officers to pull the video from the cameras situated around the river levee. In 2009, the city had installed several surveillance cameras along the three-and-a-half-mile walking path with monies from a $150,000 federal stimulus grant. The wireless cameras were situated on forty-foot-high utility poles and were generally ignored by the community, who figured the only people who needed to worry about being watched were the ones who were doing stuff they ought not be doing. It was those cameras that enabled Pendleton police to finally identify Amyjane's killer and Karen Lange's attacker.

CHAPTER THIRTY-FOUR

By that afternoon, members of the Pendleton Police Department and the Major Crime team gathered to review the events of the past twenty-four hours. As part of the process, they looked at video from the levee's surveillance cameras. They hoped that they might find Karen Lange's attacker on that surveillance footage. They didn't have to search through the tapes long.

The video recorded Karen Lange walking the parkway at 6:17 p.m. Friday, just as Dan said she was going to do. Ten minutes later, a young Asian fellow is also captured on video. He is watching Karen as she passes by. The second time she appears on the video, the fellow drops onto the pathway behind her. It's clear from the video that he is following her. He is holding what appears to be a large metal pipe behind his back. But the section of the levee where Det. Gomez found Karen in the brush has no cameras for about three hundred feet, so the man and Karen disappeared from the video. Karen never appears on camera again. There was no recording of the actual attack. At 7:29 p.m., the dark-haired man is spotted on the cameras again, about an hour after he first appeared. This time he's entering one of the levee's public bathrooms. He exits a few minutes later.

Officer Chris Freeman blurted out, "That's Danny Wu!"

"Who?" another officer asked.

"Danny Wu," Freeman said, pointing to the image on the video. "That's him."

A local transient, Danny Wu was a known entity to cops. Officer Freeman's latest interaction with Wu happened only days following Amyjane's murder. Wu was cited for illegal lodging after he was found sleeping at the levee on August 19, 2012—five days after Amyjane's murder. It was a misdemeanor citation, one that did not require Wu to be arrested or fingerprinted.

Throughout 2012 and 2013, Wu was cited for numerous offenses. Prior to 2012, police had no contact with him. Wu was arrested in one of the city parks that March for Criminal Trespass II and was booked into the county jail. In late June, he was arrested again on a warrant for failure to appear for his court date regarding the criminal trespass charge. Police had another encounter with him in mid-July, again on a criminal trespass charge. During none of those arrests or encounters did Danny Wu ever present any form of identification. He always had some excuse for why he didn't have his ID on him.

Overall, Pendleton police had twenty-seven encounters with Danny Wu during the year since Amyjane's murder. All were petty misdemeanors, dealing with homelessness. Vagrants all over this country get cited for illegal lodging, for sleeping on park benches or over the heated grates outside downtown buildings. They get cited for criminal trespassing for sneaking into park bathrooms to wash up in hours when the public traffic isn't as heavy. They have no money to defend themselves, so what's the point of showing up in court? If a warrant gets issued and they get lodged in the local jail, then at least they will get a clean bed and something to eat while they are there. It's hardly a deterrent.

The Umatilla County Jail took Wu's fingerprints in March 2013. Those fingerprints were then submitted for verification to the Oregon State Police for the Automated Fingerprint Identification

System. The second time Wu was booked, the electronic machine that scans fingerprints wasn't working, so staff at the jail made a physical copy of his fingerprints. Yet, for inexplicable reasons, or perhaps outright carelessness, Wu's fingerprints were never run through the nationwide identification system. Wu never produced any ID to verify his name, or an address. Police only knew him by the name he provided them with—Danny Wu, the name of a Chinese-American actor and martial arts expert. The only thing police knew for sure about Wu was that he hadn't grown up in the area. He had come to town from some other place.

Officer Freeman identified Danny Wu as the fellow in the video, but Chief Roberts was immediately suspicious. He didn't think Danny Wu was the vagrant's real name. Years in law enforcement and his own intuition also told him that whoever this young man was, he was likely the same man who killed Amyjane. His physical traits were just too similar to those of the fellow the motel's handyman had reported hanging around the Travelodge the day of the murder. He had to be the same killer Roberts had been losing sleep over the past year. Chief Roberts wasted no time issuing a public alert:

PENDLETON, Ore.—Pendleton police have identified the man wanted for questioning about Friday night's assault of Karen Lange, 53, along the Umatilla River walkway. Officers say Danny Wu, 23, is an Asian transient who has lived in the Pendleton area for one year. His name is unconfirmed because he doesn't have valid Oregon identification, but police are certain he is their target. Wu is 5'07", 180 lbs., with brown hair, and brown eyes. He has "Semper Fi" tattooed on the inside of his left forearm. He was last seen wearing khaki shorts and a dark brown or black t-shirt. Officers say Lange went for a walk along the parkway around 6 p.m. and was reported missing five hours later. Police later found Lange along the Umatilla River levee near Bob White field around 7:00 a.m. Saturday.

They say she was hit by a blunt object on the back of her head. An air ambulance life flighted the victim to the Oregon Health and Sciences University in Portland where she was listed in stable but critical condition as of Sunday.

The medical team at St. Anthony Hospital had determined that if Karen had any chance at all of survival, she needed more specialized care than they could provide. She would have to be air-lifted to a trauma center. Det. Gomez dispatched another officer to the Pendleton hospital with instructions to have a sexual assault exam conducted before Karen was transferred. He also asked officers to seize all her clothing, the hospital bedding, and to take clippings from her fingernails. As soon as all that evidence was collected, Karen was flown to Oregon Health & Science University in Portland. Even at Oregon's finest trauma center, doctors did not expect Karen to live through the next twenty-four hours. She was beaten so severely her skull was literally smashed in.

CHAPTER THIRTY-FIVE

Detective Jim Littlefield remembers exactly where he was on Sunday, August 18, 2013, the moment he learned that there was a DNA match between the person who assaulted Karen Lange and the person who murdered Amyjane Brandhagen. "My wife and I were coming back from a trip to the coast. We had stopped at Big Jim's Drive-In in The Dalles," Littlefield recalled. "We were eating ice cream when I got a call from the Oregon State Police crime lab. Because I had been the lead investigator on the Amyjane case, they still had me as the contact."

Littlefield was no longer with the Pendleton Police Department. He had accepted a job with the Umatilla County Sheriff's Office in early 2013. Most detectives will tell you that it's difficult to leave behind the unsolved murder cases, whether they are moving on to another job or whether they are retiring. They never quit thinking about what they might have done differently. They never quit thinking about the victim's loved ones and feeling like they have let them down somehow. Like many on this case, Littlefield had his share of sleepless nights, even after he changed departments. He was surprised to hear from the crime lab. "They said they were sorry for calling on a Sunday, but that they had found a DNA match between fingernails on Amyjane Brandhagen and the pipe used on Mrs. Lange. 'They match. The same person did both those crimes.' I was speechless," Littlefield recalled. "I was eating strawberry ice cream. I remember that." It's funny the details people remember in those clarifying moments of life. This was certainly one for Littlefield. He immediately called Chief Roberts.

"I was at home that Sunday afternoon when Detective Jim Littlefield called and relayed the crime lab's findings," Roberts recalled. "The first person I called was District Attorney Dan Primus. At the time, we had images of Wu, which is something that was absent the prior year. I was confident he would be brought to justice."

Cops who work in rural areas are more likely to have personal relationships with victims and their families. Their kids go to school together. They play ball together. They coach each other's teams. They attend the same community concerts and take part in the same bible studies. They cheer on the same bull riders at the rodeo and swell with the same pride when the flag passes by during the Round-Up parade. No one knew better than the law enforcement officers themselves how much effort had gone into finding Amyjane's killer; and, for those who worked the case, the inability to make an arrest had felt ever so much like a failure. They felt they had let their community down. So when word came that they finally had a DNA match and could positively identify a killer, Detective Littlefield and Chief Roberts were ecstatic.

Pendletonians, like most Americans, had grown accustomed to orange tag warnings scrolling across their television screens during the nightly news, the result of George W. Bush's "pay attention" policy following the attacks of 9/11. But they were not used to having a killer on the loose in their community. Angered by the threat this killer was to their generally peaceful community, locals gathered on the river levee following the assault on Karen Lange and walked the path, an act of defiance, as if to say to the murderer in hiding, *We don't fear you.* But of course, they did fear him. They especially feared him when they had no idea who he was.

On Monday, August 19th, Chief Roberts hosted a town hall at the Pendleton Convention Center. When he told the crowd of concerned citizens about the DNA link between Amyjane's killer and Karen Lange's attacker, the crowd gasped. Roberts assured them that the person who did this would be caught and brought to justice. As reported in the *East Oregonian,* Chief Roberts said, "I live in this community. If you think this hasn't haunted me every night, you're crazy."

At that very moment, Chief Roberts had no idea how very close he was to fulfilling his promise to his worried friends and neighbors. Nor did he realize how very close the killer was to all of them.

CHAPTER THIRTY-SIX

T he same day that Chief Roberts held his town hall, South African Olympic and Paralympic Star Oscar Pistorius stood in a South African courtroom and wept as the judge set his trial date for the murder of his girlfriend Reeva Steenkamp. It was also the day a statewide crime bulletin was issued regarding a manhunt for a person going by the suspected alias of "Danny Wu." The bulletin included numerous photos of "Danny Wu." There was even a close-up shot of the "Semper Fi" tattoo on his forearm, the one that matched the tattoo on the forearm of Casey Byrams, Wu's Marine buddy:

PERSON OF INTEREST: The challenge before us is finding the subject of this bullet who we know as Danny Wu. Wu is a transient who has been in the Pendleton area since August of 2012. The Pendleton Police Department has had 27 contacts with Wu in the last twelve months. All of the aforementioned contacts were the result of criminal trespass, illegal lodging, outstanding bench warrants and other violations of City Ordinance. Wu is described as a "loner" who does not associate with or talk to others. Detectives have also learned that Wu is a frequent user of public libraries. Wu typically arms himself with knives, screwdrivers and/or any device that can be used as a weapon. WU should be considered extremely DANGEROUS.[1]

Once Roberts released the bulletin, the face of "Danny Wu" was plastered all over the news, both print and electronic. Facebook and Twitter were flooded with pictures. Oregon Public Broadcasting had continued to follow the stories of Amyjane and Karen. Local TV and radio stations reported Roberts's alert, as did regional newspapers throughout the Pacific Northwest. The *Herald* in Kennewick, Washington, lead with this story:

PENDLETON—Police say DNA on a weapon used to brutally beat a Pendleton woman earlier this month matches DNA left at a 2012 murder scene. The DNA match is a break in a cold case for the Pendleton Police Department and may help them link the murder of Amyjane Brandhagen, 19, to a suspect in the recent assault, said Chief Stuart Roberts. Police have been searching for a transient who goes by the name Danny Wu since the Aug. 9 attack on Karen Lange, 53. Wu should be considered extremely dangerous and is a person of interest in both cases, police said. It's unknown if he still is living in the Pendleton or Mid-Columbia regions.

"We don't even know if Danny Wu is his true name," Roberts said. "Ultimately this guy is living a nonexistent lifestyle."

There is a warrant out for his arrest on an unrelated charge. His picture and information have been sent out to law enforcement agencies across the country.

Authorities are asking other agencies to review their unsolved attacks on women for the possibility that Wu, 23, may have been involved.

"We have been working on (Brandhagen's) case for a year," Roberts said. "To have a break on a case like this, that has left a small community like this reeling, is significant."

Surveillance footage from Aug. 9 shows Wu apparently stalking Lange with what appears to be a pipe, Roberts said.

Lange was on a nighttime walk on a trail along the Umatilla River, Roberts said.

Police found her the following morning unconscious in a brushy area with a head wound. A pipe was found nearby.

Lange remains in critical condition at Oregon Health & Science University in Portland.

The Oregon State Police forensic team said it matched DNA found on the pipe to DNA recovered at a Pendleton motel where Brandhagen was found dead Aug. 14, 2012.

Brandhagen, who worked at the motel, was stabbed several times in the chest, Roberts said. Her body was found in a room she was cleaning.

Pendleton police have contacted Wu 27 times in the past year, and he fits a description of a man seen hanging around the motel about the time Brandhagen was killed, Roberts said.

Now that the two attacks have been linked, investigators are trying to confirm if the DNA matches Wu's DNA, Roberts said. Police have personal items from Wu—a toothbrush, nail clippers and deodorant—that they will use for the tests, which could take a few weeks.

Similarities in the two attacks prompted police to test the DNA found on the pipe against the DNA found at the motel, Roberts said. Both victims were attacked in August, had the same build and both women were alone in isolated areas.

However, officials said, it doesn't appear robbery or sexual assault were motives in either case. "These were both just violent acts that left the women for dead," Roberts said.

Police haven't been able to find Wu's fingerprints in a national database, he said. Wu—who Roberts described as a "loner"—has never given police any form of identification. Attempts to track down his family or where he went to school have been unsuccessful, he said. Wu is 5-foot-7 and weighs 180 pounds. He has a tattoo on his left forearm that says *Semper Fi.* Anyone with information on Wu's whereabouts is asked to contact the Pendleton Police Department.[2]

In truth, the police didn't know Danny Wu's whereabouts or his real name. Despite a multitude of encounters over the past year, they had failed to verify his name or an address for him. Until the killer was arrested, Chief Roberts urged the community to remain diligent about their own safety and that of others. Buddy up. Walk or jog with a friend. Establish safe houses around town, so that anyone who feels threatened has a safe place to seek help. He even put patrols in golf carts around the levee.

Perhaps nowhere was the strength of the Pendleton community more evident than in the love being showered upon the Lange family. People who hadn't made prayer a part of their daily life in recent years were imploring the heavens on Karen's behalf. Dan was in Portland with Karen; he had not left her side. That Karen survived at all was, as one doctor assessed, "Not a medical miracle, just a plain miracle."

CHAPTER THIRTY-SEVEN

O nce his mug shot made the headline news, Danny Wu went into hiding. Police weren't sure if he had hitchhiked his way out of the area—Interstate 84 runs right past town—or if he was hiding out in one of the many outbuildings located on one of the many ranches surrounding town. Or maybe someone was hiding him? He had not been recorded on the video cameras around town or around the river levee since the night Karen Lange was beaten. It was almost as if he had disappeared into thin air. His fingerprints were not in any national database. Other than the DNA connecting the two crimes, and his image captured on surveillance cameras, police had very little to go on. But in that way in which God or fate or the universe sets wrongs right, it was two women who led cops to their man.

Sally Dumont and Danielle Swanson worked for Out West Catering, the premier caterer that serviced the needs of Pendleton's Convention Center. The city's main event venue hosted a slew of events throughout the year, including the city's internationally famed Pendleton Round-Up Rodeo held at the Rodeo Grounds, adjacent to the convention center. That annual event takes a year of planning and was less than a month away with lots of activities planned at the convention center leading into Round-Up.

On Wednesday evening, August 28th, around six p.m., Sally Dumont and Danielle Swanson unlocked the back door to the kitchen at the convention center and walked in on a young man sitting in a lounger drinking a Coke. "When we walked in, we realized somebody was sitting in the chair," Swanson said. "He stood up, looked at us, and said, 'I think it's time to go.'" Then, Wu grabbed his bag and headed for the center's stairwell, taking the stairs two at a time. The women recognized the killer immediately from recent news reports. They did not try to stop him. Police had warned the public that Wu was armed and dangerous, but once Wu was out of sight, the women called 911.[1] Within minutes, a couple of dozen police officers armed with assault rifles had the convention center surrounded. Umatilla County Sheriff officers even brought along a K-9 unit.

Pendleton's convention center is twenty-six thousand square feet. The adjacent rodeo grounds are even larger. Police spent over two hours peering around doorways, under bleachers, in each bathroom stall, looking in lockers and cupboards, searching for any sign of the man they knew as Danny Wu. Nothing. Dusk was afoot. They needed to find this guy before he was able to escape into darkness once again.

It was the police dog who helped find him. Wu was discovered one leg down, hanging from a hole in the convention center's ceiling. For a week or better, he'd been living in the northwest area of the building's ventilation center. With the K-9 dog barking at his foot hanging out of the ceiling, the man known as Danny Wu decided he would cooperate with police rather than be yanked out by a dog. "The dog was pretty jazzed up," Roberts said. "He didn't resist at all. No emotion whatsoever."[2] The police and the staff at the convention center, however, felt both shock and a great sense of relief. They were sure they'd caught their man.

On Thursday, August 29th, the killer appeared in an Umatilla County courtroom via video from the Umatilla County Jail where he'd been booked the previous night, following a post-arrest interview in which he matter-of-factly revealed his real name—Luke Chang. Luke was charged with first-degree murder, attempted murder, and first-degree assault for the murder of Amyjane Brandhagen and the attempted murder of Karen Lange. On Friday, August 30th, the newspaper in Luke's hometown in North Carolina, *The News Herald*, ran a front-page story on his arrest, along with a photo of police placing him handcuffed into a squad car:

Morganton man charged with murder in Oregon

Pendleton, Ore.—The slaying of a maid in a downtown Pendleton motel had stymied police for a year, until earlier this month, when surveillance cameras along a jogging path captured video of a man hiding a length of steel pipe behind his back, sneaking up on a woman who was brutally beaten.

Luke Pobzeb Chang, 23, of Morganton, was held without bail in the Umatilla County jail pending arraignment on charges of murder in the Aug. 14, 2012, stabbing of Amyjane Brandhagen, 19, in a room she was cleaning at the Travelodge in Pendleton, and attempted murder in the Aug. 9, 2013, beating of Karen Lange, 53, along the jogging path, Roberts said. While living in Morganton, Luke attended Liberty Middle School and Robert L. Patton High School.

Two officers recognized the attacker as a local homeless man who went by the name of Danny Wu. DNA from the pipe used in the attack on the jogging path matched a sample from the motel slaying, said Pendleton Police Chief Stuart Roberts. But Wu's name, fingerprints and the DNA samples did not match any nationwide databases, and while Wu's picture was circulated around the region, and there were sightings for weeks, that had all turned up empty.

On Tuesday night, workers at the local convention center spotted Wu eating leftovers in the kitchen, Roberts said. They called 911, and officers armed with assault rifles surrounded the vast building. A state trooper looking through a window spotted a leg hanging down from a ceiling in a stairwell. Confronted by officers and a police dog, the suspect came quietly, and under questioning, revealed he was a Marine Corps meteorologist, wanted for desertion after getting on a bus at Camp Pendleton, Calif., and never going back.

He apparently enlisted right out of high school in Morganton and ran out of money when he got to Pendleton, Ore. The attack on Lange and the revelation that it was linked to the Brandhagen slaying unnerved Pendleton, a high-desert town of 17,000 that is home to one of the nation's oldest rodeos, the Pendleton Roundup. The two women attended the same church, and the attacks were almost exactly a year apart, Roberts said. "It's great to have him in custody because it gives a little peace in the community," Roberts said.

Chang was cited for camping illegally along the jogging path and jailed on criminal trespass charges after repeat offenses, so officers were familiar with him, and had his fingerprints from booking him into the county jail under the name Danny Wu, Roberts said. But investigators have not uncovered any other criminal history.

A spokesman at Camp Pendleton, Lt. Ryan Finnegan, said Thursday that a person by Chang's name is listed as a deserter. Finnegan said he didn't immediately have other details about him.

And Chang did not fit the typical profile for homeless men around Pendleton. Despite harsh winters, he was better fed, cleaner, and better dressed. He seemed to have somewhere indoors to sleep, and did not appear to suffer from mental illness, alcohol or drug problems, Roberts said. But he was a loner, and regularly warned people to stay away from him, Roberts said.

After his arrest, Chang was polite, respectful, articulate and cooperative, Roberts said. Police took swabs of his DNA that are being sent to a lab for comparison with the samples from the pipe and the motel room.

Lange's husband, Dan Lange, told KGW News on Wednesday night that he was relieved by Chang's arrest. "To capture the fellow that did this is just a great relief, not only for myself and my family but for the community of Pendleton," Lange said. "What a great way to end the day."

During his arraignment hearing at the Umatilla County Courthouse via tele-conferencing from the county jail, Luke clasped his hands behind his back and stood at attention, bearing a false bravado common among Marines who've never deployed. It was as if he finally had a power over his mother Heidi and his wife Desiree that he had always craved, as if Luke was proud he had finally lived up to his granddaddy Gene's legacy.

CHAPTER THIRTY-EIGHT

The night he was arrested, Luke Chang agreed to sit for an interview with Detectives Rick Jackson and Brandon Gomez. The interview got underway shortly before eleven p.m. at the Pendleton Police Station on Airport Road.[1]

Luke seemed perfectly at ease. He wore a pair of dark pants, a blue pullover hoodie, and shackles on his wrists. His bare feet were black as tar. He fiddled with a water bottle between his shackled hands. For someone who had been living along the river for over a year, he appeared remarkably unremarkable. Other than his filthy feet, he was surprisingly well-groomed. His coarse, dark hair was neatly combed. He was small of frame, not the least bit intimidating. There was nothing about him that would alert anyone that he was a threat in any way.

The room itself was small, narrow, and institutional. A red decorative blanket hung on the wall. The blanket was a nod to the Pendleton Woolen Mills, the community's pride, and to life beyond the interview room. Detective Jackson, decked out in his camo hunting gear and a khaki cap, began the interview by pointing out to Luke that they were all being recorded by a couple of different cameras and audio devices. Luke acknowledged that he was being taped. Jackson followed up by reading him his Miranda Rights and making it clear that he did not have to cooperate. He was entitled to counsel. He did not have to sit for an interview.

"With these rights in mind, are you still willing to talk with us?" Jackson asked.

"To a certain point," Luke replied nonchalantly.

Jackson introduced Det. Gomez, who was sitting off to Jackson's left. Like Jackson, Gomez was dressed casually, a green T-shirt, jeans, and a cap. These two detectives looked like friends who were meeting for a beer. They maintained a casual composure throughout the interview, often leaning back into the stiff plastic chairs, sometimes resting their elbows on their knees. They kept a respectable distance between each other and Luke, intentionally assuming a non-threatening posture.

Jackson asked Danny Wu for his true identity.

"Luke Pobzeb Chang," he replied.

For the next hour, Jackson and Gomez got all the basics down. Luke provided his birthdate and said he'd grown up in North Carolina, where he'd been home-schooled. At eighteen, he'd joined the Marines.

"Did you see some action?" Jackson asked.

"Not at all," Luke replied. "I had an extremely boring time in the Marine Corps."

Jackson said he didn't know a lot about all that "Army stuff." He asked Luke to explain what he did in the military.

"The one job I'd signed up for was to be a weather forecaster," Luke replied. "It's an extremely tough school. They cram four years of college into nine months." He admitted he had flunked out. Most recently he was at Camp Pendleton in California but had gone AWOL in July 2012 and caught a Greyhound bus to Pendleton, Oregon.

"What brought you up this way?" Jackson asked.

"I came about it indirectly," Luke replied.

"So, you came in on the Greyhound here. What made you like Pendleton?"

"I ran out of money."

The conversation turned to why Luke didn't return to Camp Pendleton and what had prompted him to go AWOL in the first place.

"What made you want to leave?" Gomez asked.

"A stressful home situation," Luke replied in an almost verbatim quote of his grandfather's when asked why he killed a young coed.

"Explain. What do you mean?" Gomez probed.

"A wife of sorts."

"A wife of sorts?" Gomez and Jackson both laughed. "Now I'm interested."

"This one is too complicated and too personal, so I'm not going to answer that," Luke said.

"That's fine," Gomez said, waving his hand in that never-mind way.

"Were you actually married?"

"Yes."

"So, you were actually married then. Still in Camp Pendleton or is she back East?"

"I have no idea."

"You have kids?" Jackson inquired.

"No," Luke replied. "Hell, no!"

The detectives had little idea how loaded a question that was, given the nature of Luke's marriage to Desiree. It was the first hint of emotion the detectives encountered, this "Hell, no!" It was a flash point for Luke. There was anger and bitterness infused in his response.

The detectives switched gears, asking questions instead about Luke's growing up, and his family's history.

"Who's your dad?"

"Technically he's Jay Chang—Ge, but everyone just calls him Jay. He's originally from Laos. He was born over there."

"What's your mom's name?"

"Heidi Chang."

"And her maiden name?"

"Gene Lincoln."

It is interesting that when asked his mother's maiden name, Luke replied with the name of his grandfather. Not just "Lincoln." He gave his grandfather's first and last name. Jackson and Gomez were unaware of the violent history of Gene Lincoln and a possible connection to his grandson's crimes.

They didn't know about the murder of Nancy Laws or that Gene Lincoln killed a young college student after deserting his own "stressful family situation." They didn't know that Luke's grandfather had raped the young woman after he killed her. Or that Luke's grandfather drove around for a day with a dead girl's body in the trunk of a car before he buried her.

The detectives didn't know about the attempted abduction of twelve-year-old Doni Heuss and how brave she had been to fight off her attacker. Like Karen Lange, Doni lived to tell her story and to relive it. Jackson and Gomez didn't know Gene Lincoln or his impact on his grandson yet. So the question, "What's your mother's maiden name?" seemed utterly perfunctory, like when the nurse records your weight at an annual checkup.

"Gene Lincoln?" Jackson asked as he wrote it down in a little black book.

"Mmm-huh, yes," Luke replied.

Jackson reviewed what information Luke had provided so far— that he grew up in North Carolina, that he has a sibling, a younger sister, that he got married while he was in the Marines, and that because of some situation with that marriage, Luke had gone AWOL in July of 2012. Then Jackson asked about the "Semper Fi" tattoo on his wrist. Luke said, "Yeah, that tattoo. It's cursed." He noted that he got the tattoo on September 1, 2009, along with a guy named Brian and one named Casey Byrams.

"Casey Byrams. He's dead," Luke added bluntly. When he said Casey's name, Luke pulled back the sleeve on his wrist and touched the tattoo. Was he consciously inviting the detectives to explore his relationship with Casey? Or was his grief so profound even Luke couldn't explain the impact it had on him? Emotions were Luke's Achilles heel.

"How'd that happen?" Jackson asked.

"Drug overdose," Luke said.

"While he was in the Marine Corps?"

"No, this was after."

The conversation turned to Luke's daily routine in the year he'd been in Pendleton. Luke said he really liked the town. It's a great town. People didn't bug him. Luke said when he first arrived, he spent a couple of weeks at the Knights Inn, but then he started living down along the river. He would scrounge for food or whatever else he needed in trash cans around town.

"America is the most wasteful country ever," he said. "If you look in enough trash cans, if you look long enough, you'll find food." He also found blankets and clothing in dumpsters around town. "What about winter?" the detectives asked. Luke said he found a shed along the river that he stayed in. He couldn't remember where it was exactly. Throughout the interview, if the detectives came upon a detail that Luke didn't want to answer, he would either grow silent and just not answer, or he would say he couldn't remember.

"Describe an average day," Jackson implored. "What did you do? We all do something."

"Walking and reading," Luke replied.

"Reading? What do you like to read?"

"Anything I can get my hands on."

Jackson asked if Luke was into computers. Luke said no, he'd never been a techie. He hadn't even had a phone since last July.

"So, once you left the Marine Corps, you just cut off connection with everybody?"

"Yes."

"Something pretty bad had to have happened," Jackson said. There was a tension in his voice that had not been there previously.

"I'll respect what you say about not wanting to talk about your wife, whatever. But obviously something bad happened. Can I ask, did it happen to you or to her?"

"To me," Luke said.

"And that just made you say, 'I'm checking out.'"

Luke nodded, then added, "It involved my wife. She was a major part of it, but the other part of it involved my buddy who died in July."

"Casey Byrams?" Jackson asked.

"Yeah. Byrams."

Jackson asked if Luke had met any girls while he was in town, anyone he'd made friends with, anyone he took a liking to. Luke said no, he avoided people.

"I remember reading in the newspaper that I was a sociopath," Luke added. "I thought, *What does that mean?* So I looked it up. It said a person who goes out of their way to stay away from people. That's pretty much me."

"Would you describe yourself as a sociopath?" the detective asked.

"I wouldn't have before but after everything that has happened."

"Yeah, how do you feel about that?" Jackson asked.

"It fits me," Luke replied. Was Luke self-diagnosing in order to claim a label he desired? A label that he viewed as a tribute to his long-dead grandfather? Was this his way to a fame he craved?

Throughout the hours-long interview, the detectives asked Luke if he needed a bathroom break, something more to drink, or something to eat. Luke would sip from the bottled water on occasion, but he declined all other offers for a break. He did not fidget. He remained calm, controlled throughout the interview. If being interrogated made him nervous in any fashion, Luke did not show it. He didn't necessarily seem to enjoy being questioned, but he didn't appear to loathe it, either. If anything, his affect was flat, like when a parent is asking a teenager what he and his friends did last night, and the teen responds with a shrug, "Nothing."

"Why did you give police a different name?" Jackson asked, referring to "Danny Wu."

"So they can't find out about my past," Luke replied.

"Why are you now choosing to give us your real name?"

"See what happens, I guess." Luke shrugged.

"What do you think is going to happen?"

"I have no idea, but I'm curious to see what happens."

"You have a pretty good idea what's going on here, don't you?" Jackson countered.

"Yeah," Luke admitted.

"We can jump all over all night long, but you know what's going on here. This is the time when you make some life decisions on which way you want to go," Jackson said. He was leaning forward in the chair, looking directly at Luke, who did not look away. "There are some people who have been hurt by your actions. And there are some people who need answers. Would you agree?"

"Um-uh," Luke agreed.

"You mentioned that you see yourself as a sociopath. Why do you think that is so applicable to you?"

"Like the definition says, I avoid people," Luke replied.

"You have done some stuff during your time here in Pendleton that have hurt some people," Jackson reiterated. "I want to talk to you about that stuff, but I guess I want to know, will you be honest with me?"

"I'll be honest with you."

"The woman on the river levee, you know we watched you, right? You know there are cameras on the levee?"

"Mmm-uhh."

"Why did you do it?"

"Because I could," Luke answered. There was a hint of arrogance in his tone. Was he being snarky, braggadocious, or just mocking the cops?

"Because you thought you could get away with it?" Jackson pressed.

"I tried. I failed." Luke shrugged.

"And the woman when you first got here?"

"Beg your pardon?" Luke replied.

"The girl when you first got here. The one in August. Why?"

"Again," Luke replied. "To see how it felt."

"To see how what felt?" Jackson asked.

"Taking a life."

"Why?"

"I was curious."

"How did it feel?"

"Empowering," Luke said. Then, pausing, he added, "Saddening."

"Empowering and saddening? At the same time?"

"Mmm-uh," Luke said. "Empowering because I took a life. Saddening because I realized at that same time that life is precious."

"How'd you pick them? These women?"

"Crime of opportunity."

"Do you know their names?" Jackson asked. He was leaning forward in the chair, staring intently at Luke, who was still leaning back in his chair, totally relaxed.

"Yes," Luke said.

"Let's start with the first girl. Do you know her name?"

"Amyjane Nicole Brandhagen."

"Take me through that day," Jackson said.

"I woke up that day. Waited around. Walked around. Went to the library. Left the library. I didn't plan or set out to kill her. I just saw the opportunity, and I took it."

"What was the opportunity?" Jackson asked. "That's what I'm not understanding."

"She was cleaning the hotel, and the way she would clean the hotel is the rooms that needed to be cleaned, she left the doors open. I went inside one of those rooms."

"How'd you do it?" Jackson asked.

"I used a skill from my Marine Corps training."

"Which was what?" Jackson asked.

"Attack, grab, and subdue," Luke replied.

"How'd you grab her? How'd you attack her?"

"Face on. I attacked her, using my strength and skill."
"Where'd you attack her?"

"In the hotel room."

"And then what? Did you drug her?"

"No."

"How'd you get her in the bathroom?"

"The bathroom was right there," Luke said. "I just walked her in."

"How?" Jackson asked. "Were you holding her?"

"Same way you guys did me," Luke replied. "Arm behind her back."

"Then what?"

"I stabbed her with a knife."

"Where at?"

"In the chest. Multiple times."

"What position was she in?" Jackson asked. Gomez was quiet, attentive. He was leaning forward, elbows on his knees now, too.

"Flat on her back," Luke replied.

"Was she saying anything?" Jackson asked.

"Her last words, if her folks really care to know, were, 'Please, I promise. I won't tell.'" Luke repeated those words with pride, as if he were reading aloud a favorite passage of the Bible.

Luke went on to explain that when he entered the room, he had brought along a bag with extra clothes in it. After he killed Amyjane, he cleaned up as best he could and changed out of his clothes, stuffing the bloodied ones into a bag along with the knife he'd used. Then he walked out of room 231 and headed up the North Hill. He said he dumped the bloodied clothes in a garbage can and buried the knife somewhere on the North Hill. He didn't remember where.

The opportunity to attack Karen Lange was a lot more straightforward, Luke said. He saw her walking at the levee, prompting him to follow her for less than a quarter of a mile.

"I saw her, grabbed the pipe, and attacked her."

"Was there something about her that made you want to kill her?" Jackson asked.

"Not really."

"Was there something about the situation? You said these were targets of opportunity. What was it about this specific opportunity?"

"It was approaching the anniversary of the first time," Luke answered.

He explained that he'd walked at a rapid pace behind Karen Lange. When he caught up to her, he struck her with the pipe on the right side of her head.

"She dropped," Luke said.

"How many times did you hit her?" Jackson asked.

"A couple of times."

"How'd that make you feel?"

"Not as empowering as the first time," Luke admitted.

Luke said he then dragged Karen off the levee and placed her north of the river, near the baseball field. He hid the pipe, covered the blood with dirt, then changed clothes and headed to the river, where he washed up.

Luke told detectives that he had seen Karen Lange on the levee prior and had never felt any urge to try and kill her during those other encounters. But as the days drew closer to the anniversary of Amyjane's killing, he had an urge to do it again. It was that urge he was responding to, not the women themselves, or any connection they had to each other or to him.

"So you wanted to get that feeling again, get that rush?" Jackson said.

"It was not so much the rush," Luke denied, "as to see how bad I could do it and see what would happen."

"What do you mean by 'how bad'?" Gomez asked.

"I knew there were cameras. I knew they'd be watching me," Luke said.

"You wanted to be caught?"

"Yes and no. No, because obviously it's a crime and a person doesn't want to get caught doing a crime. Yes, to see how well you guys are doing."

"You were testing us?" Gomez asked.

"Yes."

"Why?" Jackson asked.

"Again, because I could."

"You feel remorse?"

"Not really."

"Why? Why is that? You've got family. Can you describe to me why you would not feel remorse about causing people pain?" Jackson asked.

"I got tired of feeling emotions and stuff like that. I got tired of being human. I got my knife. I just cut that out."

"You don't feel emotion?" Jackson asked. He sliced his hand through the air, as if he were cutting at it.

"I do feel emotion, at times, yeah," Luke said.

"So, this all had something to do with the events of getting out of the Marine Corps?"

"Yes."

"Is your wife alive?" Jackson asked.

"I don't know."

"Is homicide the only thing you like to feel?"

"Yes."

"Have you ever killed anyone else?"

"No."

"Who is the first person you killed?"

"Amyjane."

"Have you thought of killing other people?"

"Yes, of course," Luke said.

Luke said he observed other people around Pendleton and would imagine killing them, but he realized that the opportunity wasn't there; the killing wouldn't work for one reason or another. These weren't emotional decisions, Luke explained. They were decisions of logic, of analysis. The result of watching people day in and day out, observing their routines and weighing whether he could get away with the murder or not.

"Do you have a conscience?" Jackson asked.

"Yes," Luke said. "I feel bad about mistakes I've made."

"You feel bad about mistakes you've made, but these two, you don't consider mistakes?"

"No."

Wrapping up the interview sometime after midnight on August 29, 2013, Detectives Gomez and Jackson already knew they had their man. Luke's confession was taped and recorded. But it was his DNA that would positively identify him as the man who killed Amyjane and attacked Karen.

After a few more questions, Luke agreed to have his DNA swabbed. Luke's DNA, carried forward from his murderous grandfather, held more answers than the detectives realized. They were only seeking to tie it back to the DNA on the pipe used to assault Karen Lange and to the DNA collected from Amyjane's fingernails. Luke's DNA, however, also tells the story of a violent nature shared between a grandfather and a grandson.

PART THREE:

THE INHERITANCE

CHAPTER THIRTY-NINE

Those who work in law enforcement, scientists, and others who study DNA are keenly aware of the debate around nurture vs. nature, and the genetic passport that we each inherit from our ancestors. These professionals recognize there is such a thing as a "violence gene," a genetic marker that may or may not manifest depending upon various factors, both biological and environmental. Gene Lincoln did not teach his grandson Luke to kill, but his grandson may have inherited a propensity for killing from his maternal grandfather. The similarities between Gene and Luke are glaring: Both responded to "stressful family situations" by abandoning their wives and violently murdering young women they did not know. Both attempted to slay a second victim. Both failed in those second attempts. Both ended up imprisoned.

At least in Luke's case, we can be reasonably sure that this "urge to act violently" was not a learned behavior. His home environment may have been repressive, but there is no evidence it was abusive. He was taught from an early age to not act upon innate compulsions, but rather to control them: "The fruit of the Spirit is love, joy, peace, forbearance, kindness, goodness, faithfulness, gentleness and self-control. Against such there is no law."[1]

Luke's sister denies knowing about her grandfather's crimes, denies that Luke knew about those crimes, but the siblings did have contact with Gene Lincoln prior to his death in 2006. He was sixty-nine years old. How much contact and what influence that contact had remains unclear. The family is very tight-lipped about Gene's crimes and his relationship with the family once he relocated to North Carolina. A serial killer is defined as someone who commits a second homicide in which the killer has no prior relationship to the victim; and the second killing is unrelated to the first, often committed in an entirely different geographical area, and whose motive is primarily a desire to exercise power of his/her victim.[2]

Gene and Luke both possessed the makings of a serial killer, albeit both were foiled in their second attempts. Luke intended to kill Karen Lange and admitted that the thing driving him was that it was close to the anniversary of Amyjane's death. Doni Heuss remains convinced to this day that had she not fought off Gene Lincoln and escaped his car, he would have murdered her. What we don't know is if Gene Lincoln was a serial killer. Did he commit any more murders after he was released from prison only ten years after abducting Doni and murdering Nancy Laws? And once Luke is released, will he go on to commit more murders? It does not appear that the desires of a serial killer wane with time.

While many scholars and researchers identify abuse and neglect in childhood as a common component among serial killers, as far as we know, Luke's home was not wrecked by drug or alcohol abuses, adultery, child abuse, or any other societal factor typically associated with aggressive, violent behaviors. Sure, the family struggled financially, but poverty is not an uncommon thing in communities and homes throughout this country. Luke's sister Leah recalls their childhood as a time of exploration and adventure. Brother and sister roamed the woods near their home freely. The biggest tension of their childhood besides the poverty was a mother wounded by her own experiences of growing up with an alcoholic mother and a father imprisoned for a gruesome murder.

Major life events are sometimes a precursor for violent behavior, and there's little doubt that Casey's death prompted Luke's spiral. But researchers know that underneath all the external components for violence, there are biological causes at play: brain abnormalities, chemical imbalances, and DNA variants. Studies among male adoptees, for instance, show that those whose biological fathers were criminals but whose adopted fathers were not criminals displayed a higher propensity toward criminality. If the adopted father and the biological fathers both displayed violent behaviors, the male adoptee's risk for violent behavior was tripled. It is this combination of the genetic risk factors combined with the environmental risk factors that can propel a person like Luke toward a violent future.[3]

Heidi Chang responded to the chaos of her own youth by immersing herself in a restrictive religious culture whereby her life going forward could be controlled and predictable. According to Leah, Heidi was not a bad mother; she simply was a fearful one. She feared the world that she had known as a child, so she sought to raise her children in a way that she hoped would protect them. Rules and order were the fortresses Heidi constructed around her kids. Following the rules kept everyone safe. Or, at least, that was the hope and promise, right?

If Luke and Amyjane had grown up next door to each other, they almost certainly would have become good friends. People who knew both as children referred to them as "good kids." He was quiet and reserved. She was quirky and outgoing. He was thoughtful. She was kind. He was polite. She was bold. He was a reader. She was an artist. He was studious. She was adventuresome. He was a loner. She made friends of loners. He accepted the rules. She pressed against them. He felt like a misfit. So did she. He wanted to fit in, to be accepted. So did she.

Luke and Amyjane might have become the best of friends if they had met as children. However, even if such a friendship had existed, it would probably not have precluded an urge for violence that may have been latent within Luke's DNA. Growing up, Luke didn't kill animals for cruelty that we know of. He was not abusive toward his sister or his mother. The biggest complaint Leah had of her brother was that he liked to read too much. Hardly an indicator of future violent behavior.

The Christian apologist and author C.S. Lewis says in *Mere Christianity*, "When a man makes a moral choice, two things are involved. One is the set of choosing. The other is the various feelings and impulses and so on which his psychological outfit presents him with, and which are the raw material of his choice."

Like each of us, the raw material of Luke's choices may have been embedded in his DNA code. That doesn't diminish the wrongs he's done or the pain he inflicted on the community of Pendleton and upon the loved ones of Amyjane Brandhagen or Karen Lange, but as long as we as a society continue to deny the reality of a genetic propensity for violence, don't we doom people like Luke and, in essence, doom the victims of killers like Luke?

In his post-arrest interview, Luke admitted that there were many times when he felt the urge to kill but did not act upon it. He called his ability to reason his way out of murdering someone the "logical choice." But perhaps what Luke defined as "logic" was the result of his upbringing, the fact that he was raised in a home where the genetic prompts for violence were repressed and the influence to do good works and to care about others overruled his more violent nature.

"The bad psychological material is not a sin, but a disease," Lewis said. "It does not need to be repented of. It needs to be cured." We cannot help people like Gene Lincoln and Luke Chang until we understand that their issue isn't just that they need to "choose better." It's not only an issue of morality; it is an issue of molecular markers.

Every human being possesses traits that are determined by DNA: our genotypes and our phenotypes. Genotype is the genetic code of our cells, our particular blueprint, if you will. Phenotype is the physical expression of our genetic blueprint. That expression results in obvious physical ways like our eye color, hair color, height, and body shape. But phenotype isn't just about our external physical traits; it refers to our behavioral traits as well.

Consider identical twins. Their genetic blueprint—genotype—is the same. On first glance, their phenotype also appears identical: they have the same hair and eye color, similar body type and height. Yet one twin might be adventuresome, a risk-taker, while the other twin is more reserved and anxiety ridden. Our phenotype can manifest in a variety of different ways as we interact with our environment, thus producing different expressions of our genetic blueprint. While our genotype provides our "blueprint," our phenotype is the "finished building," with allowances which may include concrete poured on a rainy day or boards that fracture after they are put in place.

Up until recently, our genotype was set in ink, but all that changed when Chinese biophysicist He Jiankui used a genome-editing tool known as CRISPR to alter the genes of embryos to make them immune to HIV infection, resulting in the world's first gene-edited babies.[4] The science community was mortified that one of their own had edited embryos. Although the gene-editing tool CRISPR has been around for a couple of decades, it wasn't until 2012 that biochemist and professor Jennifer Doudna along with French professor and researcher Emmanuelle Charpentier discovered that, by using an enzyme known as Cas9, they could snip away a genome in a strand of DNA. They could also then add to those cut ends of the strand.[5] At its most basic, CRISPR-Cas9 engages a tiny battalion, or a single soldier, of RNA-messengers to repair, alter, destroy, or reconfigure genes. For their efforts, Doudna and Carpentier were awarded the 2020 Nobel Prize in Chemistry, the first women pair to ever earn such a distinction.[6]

CRISPR, a tool that edits genes, has the potential for good or evil, depending on how it is used. Employing such tools to help stop a deadly pandemic is universally praised. Using it to edit a human embryo, however, harkens back to the gothic tale of Frankenstein, and the more true-life scenario of creating a master race via designer babies. It is nothing short of terrifying. This condition is also what C.S. Lewis addressed in *The Abolition of Man*: in a scientific quest for improving the condition of mankind, it is all too natural that a man, or certain set of men, will use their power to create the next generation that will not be human at all. The only hoped-for solution, Lewis argued, is that we remain vigilant in keeping science constrained to the Tao: the fundamental and universal moral values that ensure justice for all of nature.

As the work of He Jiankui illustrates, the technology for gene editing is well ahead of society's ability to ethically constrain it.[7] One doesn't have to ponder long to understand the financial implications for using CRISPR to produce superior athletes, Herculean warriors, or killers. For all the faux outrage over biophysicist He Jiankui's revelation that he had indeed altered embryos, his work was not a secret in China or here in the US. In fact, an article titled "Chinese Scientists are Creating CRISPR Babies" appeared in the *MIT Technology Review* in November 2018. Writer Antonio Regalado noted that the Chinese had edited the first human embryos in a lab dish in 2015.

Working with a team at Southern University of Science and Technology in Shenzhen, He had published online some of the team's findings and their intention of creating embryos resistant to HIV, cholera, and smallpox. If successful, He would be responsible for a "stunning medical achievement."[8] But not one without controversy, Regalado added. "Where some see a new form of medicine that eliminates genetic disease, others see a slippery slope to enhancements, designer babies, and a new form of eugenics."[9]

In an ethics statement identifying his team's efforts, He wrote, "In this ever more competitive global pursuit of applications for gene editing, we hope to be a stand-out." Regalado's report on He's work came just ahead of the Second International Summit on Human Genome Editing. The Chinese government's reaction was less than enthusiastic. The biophysicist was sentenced to three years in prison and fined nearly $500,000. His assistants were also given prison sentences. The Chinese court ruled that in a pursuit of "fame and fortune," He had committed "illegal medical malpractice."

The question of whether humans should begin to genetically modify the unborn seems ridiculously moot given the research already underway. Science is way ahead of the public's understanding of the issues. Some might wonder if this technology wasn't purposely pursued out of the public's purview. There is, after all, ungodly amounts of money and international powers at play.

A poll conducted by Pew Research Center revealed that the bulk of Americans are amenable to some forms of gene-editing of embryos:

About seven-in-ten Americans (72%) say that changing an unborn baby's genetic characteristics to treat a serious disease or condition that the baby would have at birth is an appropriate use of medical technology, while 27% say this would be taking technology too far. A somewhat smaller share of Americans say gene editing to reduce a baby's risk of developing a serious disease or condition over their lifetime is appropriate (60% say this, while 38% say it would be taking medical technology too far). But just 19% of Americans say it would be appropriate to use gene editing to make a baby more intelligent; eight-in-ten (80%) say this would be taking medical technology too far.[10]

It is currently against the law in the US, most of Europe, and ostensibly in China to alter a human embryo. But it would be foolhardy to think that the race for a genetically engineered human isn't already underway. Which brings us back to the question of what about Gene Lincoln and his grandson Luke? If we could edit a human embryo to remove the urge to murder, should we? What are the implications of that? If we can edit out the urge to murder, wouldn't it be equally as easy to insert into a human embryo the urge to kill?

CHAPTER FORTY

It rubs most Americans the wrong way to even consider the scientific evidence of a genetic component to violence. Police Chief Stuart Roberts doesn't believe that under our current system of governance, we are willing to address the issue. "I have a lot of thoughts about genetic predisposition," Roberts said. "Unfortunately, US law enforcement, the courts, and society have not been willing to consider or embrace the science that would allow criminal, civil, and social justice to become more progressive and preventative in nature versus being almost entirely reactive."

Society has a primarily punitive approach to dealing with violence, rather than a thoughtful, considered approach. Our inability to accept scientific evidence that a DNA component for violence exists in no way diminishes the fact that it does exist. That's the great thing about facts—they don't care whether you believe them to be true or not. They just go right on about the business of being true.

However, genes don't act in isolation. There is an ever-expanding body of research into the effects of trauma upon DNA. While trauma will not change the DNA code itself, each gene has its own control panel that can be damaged as a result of trauma. Imagine taking a hammer to your laptop. If you beat the keyboard with the hammer, the keyboard will still exist in an altered form, but it will no longer function the way it was intended. Trauma can act like a hammer to a person's genomes. Such modifications to the gene can and do have lasting effects on human health and behaviors.

We are used to blaming environmental factors such as neglect, poverty, and low socio-economic environment as indicators for those who are predisposed to criminal behavior. We shun the notion, however, that a person's DNA may be a contributing cause of criminal behaviors. In a society built upon the notion of free will and being self-determinant, we mistrust the idea that a person can be predisposed toward violence, the way they may be predisposed to diabetes or cancer.

Part of this reluctance is because of the misuse and outright abuse of early gene studies. The global eugenics movement was nothing more than a way of oppressing the oppressed and elevating the already privileged. Eugenicists sought to achieve a better society with "desirable" gene characteristics by breeding out "undesirable" gene traits. It was wrong one hundred years ago and remains wrong today.

Consequently, scientists have been reluctant to talk openly in the public forum about the existence of an aggression gene simply because they seek to steer clear of the racially motivated eugenics movement. Who can blame them? It is important to remember that each of us is a mottled mess of genes, each with a sensitive epigenetic control center. We are a conglomeration of the DNA we inherit from our parents, and their histories, and the trauma our ancestors endured, along with the environment in which we are raised.

Dr. Kevin Beaver, the Judith Rich Harris Professor of Criminology at Florida State University, is well-versed in the debate over the underpinnings of violent behavior. While the general public may not be aware, Beaver said, "the argument of Nature vs. Nurture has been long settled. It is both the result of our genes and our environment."[1] Dr. Beaver recognizes the reluctance, sometimes even within the academic community, to acknowledge a genetic component to violence: "There are a lot of people who say genes don't matter. They don't want to talk about genes for crimes because they don't want to get into eugenics. But if you look at things scientifically at all, every study shows a link between violence and genes. For serious kinds of crimes—the extremes in behavior—we tend to see that genetic affect even more prevalent, as high as 70 percent and higher."

Thus, the genetic line of a serial killer is more likely to have a predisposition toward violence and aggression. This does not mean that the child of a killer is predestined to kill, any more than being the child of a diabetic ensures that the child will become a diabetic. The propensity toward diabetes may be within that child's DNA, but a person can combat those genetic influences through eating right and exercising.

The difference is that when it comes to illnesses like diabetes, we are more than willing to accept that there is a genetic predisposition and to use that information in ways that lead to better health. Whereas, when it comes to the notion of a DNA variant for violence, as a society we are completely failing to take a proactive approach. We are abandoning those most at risk to deal with their genetic mishaps in isolation, which heightens the possibility that they will turn to violence. Perhaps the reason Luke Chang was a loner is because he feared his own impulses and urges, the ones driven by the hereditary gene for violence passed down through his mother's line.

"We mark crime up to the usual suspects: family, poverty, culture. You never hear a person say, 'It's in the genes,'" Dr. Beaver said. "It's always environmental and social causes. We stifle public debate around genetics and crimes, and this, ultimately, handicaps us for prevention and rehabilitation of offenders. If there is a strong genetic affect for crime, what are the policy implications? That's a brave new world perspective."

It's a perspective we may not be willing to consider yet, despite the evidence. Consider if you will that when we visit a doctor's office we are asked to provide our family's medical history. Just filling out such a form is a recognition that there are genetic markers that may affect our overall well-being. Scientists from the Karolinska Institute in Sweden conducted a study of almost nine hundred criminals in Finland and found that the most violent ones, those who had committed ten or more homicides or attempted homicides, carried the MAOA low-activity genotype.[2] Researchers said that the enzyme deficiency could cause a sort of dopamine hyperactivity, which would be exacerbated by drinking or drugs.[3] Keep in mind that in the months leading into the murder of Amyjane, Luke was drinking and using the synthetic drug Spice.

Spice is a synthetic cannabinoid, but unregulated, there is no telling what the chemical compound contained. Spice has been known to cause psychotic episodes, rapid heart rate, panic, psychosis, difficulty breathing, and even loss of life. Desiree Chang said that Luke's Spice habit had gotten totally out of control. She thought the bulk of his income was going toward buying Spice. We have no indication that he was using at the time he killed Amyjane, but there is also no way to determine how the chemical compound affected his already compromised DNA. Could it be that Luke's Spice habit was like taking a mallet to his genomes?

Perhaps it is time to take seriously the truth that Dr. Beaver points out: "There is now an impressive amount of empirical research produced by behavioral geneticists indicating that virtually every single human behavioral phenotype is the result of a complex arrangement of genetic and environment factors. A body of research has revealed that virtually all antisocial phenotypes are influenced to varying degrees by genetic factors."

Ongoing twin studies have likewise supported a significant hereditary link.[5] Dr. Kent Kiehl, a professor of Neuroscience and Law at the University of New Mexico, conducted brain-imaging studies on four thousand criminals. His research suggests that the brains of psychopaths are physically different. Genetics accounts for at least 50 percent of the physical differences of a psychopath's brain, including less gray matter and smaller amygdala.[4] The amygdala is that part of the brain that affects decision-making and our emotions.

Leah described Luke as distant emotionally. She doesn't know if he has ever felt any sorrow, or sought forgiveness for killing Amyjane and for attempting to kill Karen Lange. She has never discussed Luke's violent actions with him. "I have found all the what-ifs to be an endless pit of despair," Leah said. "I've had to accept his choices and love him for who he is."

Hopefully, the more we learn about DNA and its implications, the better able we will be at addressing issues of genetic inheritability. We know for a fact that there is a breast cancer gene that is passed through the maternal line. That knowledge enables women to make better decisions about their own breast health. By the same token, we know that crime runs in families. Author Fox Butterfield highlights the criminology of one extended family. Referring to a particular study out of England, Butterfield noted that there was evidence of an "intergenerational transmission of violence."[6] Just as being a teacher or a doctor or an engineer runs in families, so do criminals.

Butterfield maintains policymakers have been unwilling to address the issue, choosing instead to be punitive instead of proactive. "University of Maryland criminologist John Laub told me it's because any suggestion of a possible biological or genetic basis for crime could be misconstrued as racism. Instead," Butterfield noted, "researchers have looked at other well-known risk causes like poverty, deviant peers at school, drugs, and gangs." Butterfield considers the $182 billion-a-year US criminal justice system egregiously flawed. "The more people we lock up the more people we have to lock up." But Butterfield cautioned against the idea of an "immutable crime gene."[7] Every single day in this country, a child of a killer determines that they will not surrender their will to whatever criminal urges may befall them. They will rise above that—the way Leah has done. The way Casey Byrams' siblings have done.

Luke had an urge to kill, but he did not have to act upon that urge and at many points chose not to. He admitted to Detectives

Gomez and Jackson that he had considered killing other people but had reasoned his way out of doing so. He could have made the same choice with Amyjane and with Karen. But it would be wrong not to acknowledge that Luke had more factors at play in his decision to murder than free will. Given that there is substantial evidence of a genetic component to the criminology of families, shouldn't that at least be a consideration for how we can better help people like Luke Chang, to deter them from their more violent inclinations?

We can and should hold Luke accountable to the egregious wrongs he has done. But should we not also consider that we, too, continue to play a part, by failing to consider that what Luke lacked wasn't just enough will power to choose better, but a flawed DNA code as well?

The murder gene appears to be transgenerational.

Some kids inherit their grandparent's ranch or their beach house. Some kids inherit their grandparent's musical aptitude or their athletic prowess. Some kids inherit their grandparent's bushy eyebrows or big ears. Yet, it seems an unfortunate few like Luke Chang inherit their grandfather's murder gene.

EPILOGUE

On a cold January day in 2014, former Marine Luke Chang, twenty-three, took his place before Umatilla County Judge Lynn Hampton and entered a guilty plea for the murder of Amyjane Brandhagen and for the brutal beating of Karen Lange.

"He is ready to face the music," said Luke's court-appointed attorney.

Luke stood silent before the judge, his hands and feet shackled. He wore a yellow jumpsuit, courtesy of the taxpayers of Umatilla County. His dark hair, thick and shaggy, curled slightly around his ears. He offered no apology to the court.

No one came to offer him support of any kind. No family. No friends. No loved ones of any sort. His parents sent a letter to him from the Taiwan mission field where they continue to serve. "We love you" was all they wrote. Even his sister did not make the trek from her home in Southern California. Nor did his wife. Desiree had not spoken with Luke or heard from him since that phone call when she told him Casey was dead. Whether Luke felt abandoned in that moment or not, only he knew. As usual, his face was void of any noticeable emotion, as blank as an empty plate.

Judge Hampton, however, was obviously distressed. Like most everyone in Pendleton, she, too, knew the Brandhagen family, knew of Amyjane and of Karen Lange. Her hands clasped before her, Judge Hampton did not flinch as she studied Luke for some sign of remorse, regret, any hint of empathy on his behalf. He offered her none. "There's no way this sentence will make up for the loss to this community, but you have thirty-five years to think about that," Judge Hampton said as she sentenced the killer.

It was a plea deal, offered by District Attorney Dan Primus. Initially, upon his arrest, Luke had entered a plea of not guilty by reason of insanity. The community was outraged by the plea deal. Luke was sentenced to twenty-five years for the first count of murder and ten years for the second count of attempted murder. Primus felt comfortable with the fact that Luke would not be eligible for parole until he turns fifty-eight.

At the Oregon State Penitentiary in Salem, Oregon, Luke is Inmate 20010809. He and Leah speak on occasion. Luke's routine is pretty much the same day in and day out. Leah, however, has fallen in love, gotten married, moved away from Southern California. She has a life she enjoys. Her parents have been to see her brother. She has not.

Despite my requests, Luke declined to be interviewed for this book, stating in a letter to me that there was nothing for him to gain by participating.

Desiree left California and moved back to Cullman for a while. She enrolled at the local community college. She has a daughter by another Marine. Her daughter is bright and beautiful and seemingly free of the health problems that continue to beset her mother. Desiree obtained a divorce from Luke. She has no contact with him. She has not remarried. Her health coverage is through the state's assistance program. Her mother, devoted as ever, steps into the gaps in caring for her daughter and her granddaughter. "My mom is doing everything in her power to help me," Desiree says. She still deals with guilt from time to time over Luke. She knows that he loved her in ways she could never love him. She feels like if she hadn't needed the health insurance so badly, they would never have married. Maybe if they hadn't married, he would never have flipped out and killed Amyjane. Like Leah said, it's the "what-ifs" that cause Desiree and others to spiral into despair. It's better not to go there.

Megan Keel is also back in Cullman. She was not welcome at Casey's funeral, even though they were still married at the time of his death. There are a lot of hurt feelings, as is often the case in these situations. Megan, too, feels bad about what happened with Luke, who, she said, "would give you the shirt off his back if you needed it." The thought that Luke could kill anyone was so totally unimaginable to her. "He was the sweetest guy." Megan still misses Casey. Theirs was a love that might have lasted a lifetime if only they were older, more mature, more disciplined, and more financially stable. The "if-onlys" are as difficult to deal with as "what-ifs."

Doni Heuss is a grandmother now. Her children and grands know a little bit about the courage of their mother and grandmother, how she escaped certain death from the hands of a killer. Doni is happily married to a man who has loved and appreciated her strength. She has retired from the janitorial job at the community college where she worked nights. Sometimes, while working in the quiet halls or classrooms, she would feel a chill, as if she was being watched, stalked, the way she was that morning she was abducted all those years ago. The name of Gene Lincoln still evokes fear in her although he's long dead. Doni marvels that the young girl she was in the summer of '73 had the strength and presence of mind to fight off a would-be killer. "God was with me," she says.

Karen Lange also attributes her own survival to God and the prayers of the community of Pendleton and to those from around the world. She was not expected to live. Doctors told her husband that. Luke Chang had beat on Karen with a metal pipe and left her for dead. He fractured her skull. She was hidden in brush off the walkway, bleeding out for nearly thirteen hours.

Thankfully, Karen has little memory of the attack. She remembers going out for a walk and waking up in the hospital. She was hospitalized in Portland for months, not returning to her Pendleton home until November following the August attack. Her husband, Dan, was at her side throughout her healing, documenting the tiniest bit of progress for their sons, then eighteen and twenty-one, and for all the people praying. "I'm waiting expectantly and hopefully and praying for Karen to begin making cognitive responses—move fingers, wiggle toes, squeeze a finger, sing a song," he blogged, two weeks after her attack.

Nothing about Karen's healing came quickly. It was all incremental, like watching a newborn discover the world—first lights, then faces, then fingers, then toes. It was nearly a month before Dan got so much as a brief smile from his wife. Still, he remained hopeful, encouraging, always praying, always trusting, always believing that God would use all this pain in a redemptive way. Without this suffering, Dan believed that the killer might remain free. It was Karen Lange's attack that enabled police to identify Amyjane's murderer.

Yet, even amid it all, Dan said he bore no ill will toward Luke Chang. "He has demons he wrestles with," Dan said. "Karen will recover, and this individual will spend the rest of his life with what he did. I do not envy him. We can move on with the rest of our lives."

Karen did recover. She returned to work and even recovered well enough to sing the National Anthem at the Opening Ceremonies of the Pendleton Round-Up a year later. It was, she said, a way of giving back to the community who had stood beside her and her family.

The terror that a murderer had inflicted upon the City of Pendleton was broken by the strong and steady voice of Karen Lange echoing throughout Round-Up stadium as cowboys and cowgirls, and even city folks from around the country, rose to their feet, wildly cheering for the miracle standing before them.

AUTHOR'S NOTE

The idea of this book began over coffee with Pendleton Police Chief (Ret.) Stuart Roberts in the months following the murder of Amyjane Brandhagen, long before Luke Chang made a second murder attempt. It was during our meeting that Chief Roberts revealed his fear that they might be dealing with a serial killer. By some definitions, a serial killer is someone who has committed two or more murders. While neither Luke nor his grandfather quite meet that standard, I believe that had they not been apprehended, they most definitely would have gone on to kill again. Both attempted to, and without question, both possessed a desire to kill. Luke discussed his desire to kill with detectives. One wonders, however, if they both didn't want to be caught on some level. Their second attempts were so clumsy and obvious, it was as if a side of them were begging to be stopped.

Following my meeting with Chief Roberts in 2012, I petitioned the city attorney for access to the police records under the Freedom of Information Act. That petition was granted, and I began a nearly decade-long journey of uncovering the story of Luke Chang. This book was never a whodunit, but rather a why'd he do it. It would have been helpful if Luke would have sat down with me and explained how he transformed from the good missionary's child to the killer he became. That would have been every writer and every reader's dream scenario, but with killers like Luke, control is their power.

He responded to my written request for an interview in March 2016 with a handwritten note on lined notebook paper with the opening sentence: "This letter is one of refusal." He writes in print, not cursive, with little flourishes. The way an eighth-grade boy would write a paper when he is trying to get at least a B-grade. In his letter of decline, Luke added, "I find it quite unusual that people want to know about my case." There's insight in that statement. Even as I wrote this book, I never referred to it as anything but the case of Amyjane Brandhagen. I never once considered it the case of Luke Chang. Yet he does. I'll leave any judgments about that to readers to discern.

Luke ends his letter with a curious line: "Your letter was vague about your intentions, vague about your knowledge of me, and also vague about what you intend to do with that knowledge." The letter I wrote to him was straightforward: I asked for an interview to discuss a book I was writing about the murder of Amyjane Brandhagen. Was he including this statement because he was curious and maybe interested in meeting? Any notion along those lines was cut off by the very next statement: "Please do not contact me any further in the future." It's notable that he signed it "Sincerely" and then in pen scribbled out his name, as if writing in pen formalized matters.

Once the Pendleton's city attorney approved my FOIA request, I was given a room at the Pendleton Police Department and spent a couple of weeks going through the case files, asking questions of detectives who covered the case, probing Chief Roberts for follow-up information. Pendleton Police Department assistant Dianna Anderson was particularly helpful in tracking down documents, files, photos, videos, and anything else I needed related to the investigation. It was while reading through some of the case files that I learned about the relationship between Casey Byrams and Luke. My initial read just showed Casey's name among many people associated with Luke. But what jumped out at me was the Casey was from Cullman, Alabama, a place I had been to many times in my work as an author.

I was first introduced to Cullman by fellow journalist Loretta Gillespie. A local columnist for the *Moulton Advertiser*, Loretta reached out and invited me to do an author's talk about my previous true crime book, *A Silence of Mockingbirds* (MacCadam/Cage, 2010). During that first visit, Loretta and I discovered we had much in common and became fast friends. Over the years, I've returned to Cullman and to the book events Loretta sponsors at her home in Moulton. We often make sure to include author events at Berkley Bob's Coffee House in nearby Cullman as well. When I discovered that Luke had contacts with people in Cullman, I immediately reached out to Loretta. With her help, I was able to track down Casey's family, as well as Desiree.

Science may have been my first love as I was picking up seashells as a young girl on Oahu's North Shore or Florida's Gulf Coast, but years of education left me feeling completely inadequate in the pursuit of it. I believe my fate in the sciences was sealed when my high school teacher threw an eraser at my head for asking him to please explain atoms. So please appreciate my rudimentary understanding of DNA. I've taken a novice's approach of trying to tackle a difficult subject matter in order to raise questions, not provide answers.

Many people have helped me through the writing of this book. First and foremost, thank you to the publishing team of Koehler Books for making my work better. Thank you Jessica Meigs, Kellie Emery, Ariana Abud, and Joe Coccaro for adding your talents to this work. Big hugs of huge thanks to my dear friend Susie Stuvland and to Mikal Wright of the Pendleton Round-Up Association and Happy Canyon Company for helping with the cover design. Thank you to early readers Debbie Johnson, Mike and Tammy McCullough, and Loretta Gillespie. Thank you to the court clerks in Umatilla County, Oregon; Baraga County, Michigan; Newago County, Michigan, for helping me track down records. Thanks also to those who welcomed me into New Manna Baptist Church, and although rightfully skeptical, met with me anyway and provided much-needed insight into the Chang family dynamics.

I owe a debt of gratitude to Doni Heuss, who tepidly recounted her story of the day Gene Lincoln abducted her at knifepoint. As you might imagine, this is a deeply disturbing story for Doni, and she has only shared it with a handful of people. I have the utmost respect and awe at the strength of that twelve-year-old girl that lives within Doni. Gene Lincoln thought he could subdue a child with relative ease. He had no idea of the fire that flames within Doni Heuss. Had it not been for Doni, Nancy Laws's killer may never have been arrested. That Gene Lincoln spent so little time in prison for the murder of Nancy Laws and the abduction of Doni Heuss is a telling commentary on how our legal system diminishes the lives of women and young girls. When men are making all the deals, it is not women who are well-served. Just ask the victims of Larry Nasser.

Prior to his death in 2018, I spoke with Fred Bralich, husband of Nancy's sister Judy. Fred told me that Judy, who had already passed, would have been happy to have someone looking into the story of her sister's death. "She never got over it," Fred said. Judy had long felt that the prosecutors had done her family wrong in pushing a plea deal for Gene Lincoln. The loved ones of murdered victims have a particular kind of grief journey that only those who have lived it can begin to appreciate.

It is with much gratitude that I say thank you to Pendleton Police Chief (Ret.) Stuart Roberts, Umatilla County Undersheriff Jim Littlefield, Pendleton Police Detective Sgt. Rick Jackson, and Pilot Rock Police Chief Bill Caldera. Your dedication to law enforcement and to the community at large helped right the wrongs done to Amyjane Brandhagen and Karen Lange. It is my hope that this story helps enlighten the community about the enormous tasks you undertook in bringing about justice.

A special thank-you to my writing peers, who encouraged me along over the decade I've worked on this project. A special shout-out to author Michael Morris who served as a sounding board for this project. Additionally, thank you to my family and the multitude of readers who cheer me on daily. Y'all are all invited over for coffee and pie.

And to Tim, who never ever lets me quit, no matter the cost to him personally, thank you for being my Ted Lasso and always believing in me and the work I do.

ENDNOTES

The notes that follow are not academic in nature. I offer them as an aid to help readers understand the process of my investigation. They serve more as a roadmap. The designated page numbers reveal the source of the information on that page or the pages following. I had no idea when I began my investigation how extensive a story this would become, or the scientific research that it would require. Information gathered may continue beyond the page cited, just as a road might continue past the turn. Look to further reading for an understanding of some of the background material that helped inform me as I wrote.

PROLOGUE

1. *Barbara Loden: A Woman Telling Her Own Story Through That of Another Woman*, R. Brody, *The New Yorker*, Nov. 1, 2016.

2. Interview, phone call, correspondence with Pastor Jason Garner and Trisha Garner, New Manna Baptist Church, March 2019.

CHAPTER ONE

1. Interview, correspondence, Shane Jarvis, Morganton, North Carolina, March 2019.

2. Cacti, Kyoto. *Bamboonery,* June 2011, http://kyotocacti.blogspot. com/2011/06/bamboonery-.

3. Mission statement and letter from Jay and Heidi Chang, http:// gochristianhelps.com/othmiss/Chang.htm.

4. Van Boom, Daniel. "Scientists are discovering the secrets behind whole-body regeneration." March 17, 2019.

5. Young, Kevin W. *The World of Broadus Miller: Homicide, Lynching and Outlawry in Early Twentieth-Century North and South Carolina,* Doctoral Dissertation, University of Georgia. Athens, Georgia, 2016.

CHAPTER TWO

1. Interviews with Pendleton Police Chief Stuart Roberts, 2013-16. It was shortly after Amyjane's death that I reached out to Pendleton Police Chief Stuart Roberts. We had worked together on my previous true crime book—*A Silence of Mockingbirds*—about the murder of three-year-old Karly Sheehan. This meeting at Hamley's was the first of many to occur over the next few years as the story of Luke Chang unfolded. It was at this very first meeting that Roberts first expressed his concern that whoever killed Amyjane could be a total unknown in the area. He had a sense from the start that he was dealing with a serial killer. Throughout all my dealings with him, Chief Roberts was always circumspect and professional. He retired from Pendleton Police Department in 2020.

CHAPTER THREE

1. Garrod, A E. "The incidence of alkaptonuria: a study in chemical individuality. 1902." *Molecular medicine (Cambridge, Mass.)* vol. 2,3 (1996): 274-82.

2. Genome News Network, Craig Venter Institute. *Archibald E. Garrod postulates that genetic defects cause many inherited diseases, 1908.*

3. Schwarzbach E., Smykal P., Dostal O., Jarkovska M., Valvoa S. (2014); *Gregor J. Mendel – Genetics founding father.* Czech J. Genet, Plant Breed., 50:43-51.

4. Maddox, Brenda. *Rosalind Franklin: The Dark Lady of DNA.* New York City, Harper Perennial, 2003.

5. Richardson, Sarah. "A Violence in the Blood." Discover, 23, Sept. 1993.

6. Richardson, Sarah. "A Violence in the Blood. Discover, 23, Sept. 1993.

7. Oubre, Alondra. "The Extreme Warrior Gene: A Reality Check." Scientia Salon, July 31, 2014.

8. Vevera, Jan et. al. "Rare Copy Number Variation in Extremely Impulsively Violent Males." *Genes, Brain, and Behavior,* vol.18, 6 (2019). http://pubmed.ncbi.nim.nih.gov/30411505/.

CHAPTER FOUR & CHAPTER FIVE

1. The scenes in these chapters are inspired by the following newspaper reports and photos regarding the missing woman, Nancy Laws, and subsequent court records of the firsthand account from Gene Lincoln:

"City Woman Missing." *Waukesha Daily Freeman*, 18 June 1973.

Kaste, Ivan. "Michigan Discovers Suspect in Case of Missing Waukesha Woman." *Waukesha Daily Freeman*, 2 August 1973.

"Wide Search for City Woman Fails." *Waukesha Daily Freeman*, 3 August 1973.

Ruckert, Tom. "Woman's Hobby May Have Led to Her Harm." *Waukesha Daily Freeman*, 6 August 1973.

Kaste, Ivan. "Another Clue Told on Missing City Woman." *Waukesha Daily Freeman*, 16 August 1973.

The County of Baraga and the People of the State of Michigan vs. Gene Dale Lincoln, p.1-45, 13 November 1975.

CHAPTER SIX

1. I tracked Doni Heuss down in 2014 through a family member. When I identified myself as an author, Doni knew immediately why I was calling: "Gene Lincoln," she said. Doni worked a job that placed her alone in the evening. Even though he was dead by the time of our first conversation, Gene Lincoln still haunted her. She had a difficult time shaking her fear of him, and understandably so. Doni rarely ever spoke about the day that she was abducted, but she graciously worked with me on this project, answering every question I put to her. I firmly believe had Doni not fought Lincoln off that day, he would have killed her and gone on to kill again. Doni believes that, too. She is the one shining light that helped propel this story forward.

CHAPTER SEVEN

1. "Decal on Window Helped Locate Missing Waukesha Woman's Auto." *Waukesha Daily Freeman,* 11 August 1973, White Cloud, Michigan.

CHAPTER EIGHT

1. Interview with Douglas Springstead, 20 February 2018.

2. Lindt, Terry. "It's Over, says Sister of Murdered Woman." *Waukesha Daily Freeman,* 7 Sept. 1973.

3. State of Michigan vs. Gene Dale Lincoln, 7 September 1973.

4. Transcripts. State of Michigan vs. Gene Dale Lincoln, 13 Nove. 1973; 14 Nov. 1973; 29 January 1974.

CHAPTER NINE

1. "Man Admits Murder of Woman, 24." *Ironwood Daily Globe,* 7 Sept. 1973.

2. "Charges Disputed for City Woman's Slayer." *Waukesha Daily Freeman,* 20 Nov. 1973.

3. Kaste, Ivan. "City Woman's Slayer Gets 10 to 15 years." *Waukesha Daily Freeman,* 30 Jan. 1974.

4. Transcripts. State of Michigan, Baraga County vs. Gene Dale Lincoln. 29 Jan. 1974.

CHAPTER TEN

1. Insights into the family and family history and Luke, specifically, were provided in interviews with Leah Chang, Luke's sister, from 2014-2018. These interviews took place by phone and through social media messaging. Jay and Heidi Chang are missionaries. They have spoken at various churches, giving testimony about their faith journey, which includes their past. They did not respond to interview requests. I also gained background information from the following articles: Wright, Phil. "Marine Deserter and Murder Suspect Lukah Chang is Son of Christian Missionaries." *East Oregonian*, 30 August 2013; and Wright, Phil. "Brother, Killer, Mystery." *Blue Mountain Eagle*, 27 Feb. 2014.

2. "What to do in the Storm." Vimeo, Ge (Jay) Chang, Pacific Bible Church, 2016. GodChrisitanHelps.org http://www.gochristianhelps. com/othmiss/Chang.htm.

3. "Who was Jack Hyles? A Look into His Life & Ministry" http:// jackhyleslibrary.com/about-jack- hyles/.

4. Janega, James. "Rev. Jack Hyles: Led Bus Ministry." *Chicago Tribune*, 9 Feb. 2001.

5. Smith, Bryan. "Let Us Prey: Big Trouble at First Baptist Church." *Chicago Magazine*, 11 Dec. 2012.

6. Vang, Xou..." "Dr. Vang PobZeb". *Learn Hmong Lessons and Traditions*. http://hmonglessons.com.

7. King James Bible, *The Great Commission*, Matthew 28:16-20.

CHAPTER ELEVEN

1. Herndon, Nancy. "A New Life in the 'land of opportunity'. Relocated Hmong refugees make a home for themselves in rural

North Carolina." *The Christian Science Monitor*, June 11, 1987.

2. Conversations with Leah Chang took place over several years. Direct quotes are from the notes during those conversations or exchange of correspondences. Familial relationships are as Leah defined them. Background information was gleaned from Leah and other family members who did not want to go on the record for personal reasons. These conversations with Leah are interspersed throughout the book. Bear in mind, however, that how Leah felt about her brother's crimes or how she may have felt about her mother at the time of our conversations may have changed over time. There did come a point, not long after Trump's election, when Leah did not want to communicate anymore. She left California where she had been living and working and moved to Arizona. Since her move, Leah has cut off contact with the author. There was no reason given. There was no prior notice or any indication that she no longer wished to cooperate with the telling of this story. Like most posts in 2015, it came across as very politicized. Had Luke asked Leah to stop talking?

CHAPTER TWELVE

1. "NC law makes cockfighting felony." *WISNEWS 10*, Sept. 29, 2005.

2. Correspondence with Lewis Lincoln, Gene Lincoln's son and Heidi Lincoln's brother.

CHAPTER FOURTEEN

1. The information on Casey Byrams came through interviews with Casey's mother, Charlotte; Megan Keel, his estranged wife; and Desiree Chang, a friend; as well as newspaper reports and police reports. I also interviewed some of those soldiers who served alongside Casey, including his superior.

2. Senator Garlan Gudger told me the story about his encounter with Katie Couric on one of my visits to Cullman.

3. Interviews and correspondence with Megan Keel.

CHAPTER FIFTEEN

1. Kessler Air Force Base: Marine Detachment Mission: https://www.keesler.af.mil.

CHAPTER SIXTEEN

1. Interviews and correspondence with Desiree, 2013-2019. At the start of our correspondence/interviews, Desiree was seeking a divorce from Luke Chang, which she eventually obtained. Desiree, like Doni, was forthcoming about some very painful memories. We spoke by phone, email, and messaging. She still lives with the aftermath of Luke's choices. The impact of his choices upon his victims continues to have a daily impact, even years later.

CHAPTER EIGHTEEN

1. Interview and correspondence with Sgt. Thomas Joyce. Joyce clearly thought the world of Casey. He knew of Casey's struggles with depression and felt a kinship with Casey that he did not with Luke. He knew who Luke was but never really had much of a relationship with Luke the way he did with Casey. During our conversations, he told me how his own childhood had marred by a murder. Casey's death left Sgt. Joyce wondering what more he might have been able to do to help prevent the outcomes for both Casey and Luke. But as we all know, we don't get to control the behaviors of others. What was clear to me was Sgt. Joyce's integrity and his deep concern for Casey and Luke.

2. Rodriquez, Frank. "Spice: The cheap cannabis imitator has dangerous side effects." *Borderzine: Reporting from Across the Fronteras*, Dec. 27, 2012. https://borderzine.com.

CHAPTER NINETEEN

1. Interview and correspondence with Keith Keel, Megan's dad, and Casey's father-in-law.

CHAPTER TWENTY-TWO

1. Police report, Pendelton Police Department. Interview with Amyjane Brandhagen's neighbors.

CHAPTER TWENTY-FOUR

1. All information regarding the crime scene at Pendleton's Travelodge came from police reports provided by Pendleton Police following a FOIA request to Pendleton's city attorney, and from interviews with those involved in the investigation. Pendleton police were professional and cooperative throughout the development of this story. This included crime scene photos and video as well as individual officers' reports and supplemental reports for Case #12-2770.

2. Lt. Bill Caldera recalled the events of the investigation with me via telephone and email. So in addition to having the police reports, I did speak with various investigators involved in the case. Lt. Caldera was one.

3. Wilson, Michael, "Killed by a Stranger: A Rare Event but a Rising Fear." *New York Times*, August 17, 2016.

CHAPTER TWENTY-FIVE

1. Interviews with Detective Jim Littlefield via phone and email.

CHAPTER TWENTY-EIGHT

1. The information on Sullivan Jim comes from the police reports and interviews with those who worked the investigation. I reached out to Sullivan Jim for an interview, but we never connected.

CHAPTER TWENTY-NINE

1. Amyjane's autopsy report was included in her case file information I obtained through FOIA.

CHAPTER THIRTY-TWO

1. Police reports regarding FBI contact with C. Tackett. I also corresponded with Tackett re: his relationship with Amyjane. Tackett no longer goes by the name Amyjane knew him as but rather the name Skye Warden.

CHAPTER THIRTY-THREE

1. The information on Karen Lange was drawn from various news reports in the *East Oregonian*, *The Oregonian*, and Oregon Public Broadcasting, as well as FOIA police reports. Additionally, Dan Lange provided updates online and available to the public. I did reach out to Karen Lange for an interview, and she initially agreed, but after consultation with others withdrew her participation. She provided no reason for that, except to say her memory was limited due to the

attack. Karen Lange was always gracious. It should also be noted that I did reach out to Amyjane's parents as well, inviting them to participate, but it's clear why they declined. They wanted to preserve their daughter's memory, as is their right to do. They did, however, reach out to a mutual friend who passed along the message that they were "worried" I might investigate this story. Facts have a way of shattering the exteriors we hide behind. I get it, but falsehoods serve no one well in the long run. While I don't assume that I have every fact correct, I have done my due diligence to tell as truthful a story about the murder of Amyjane Brandhagen as I had access to. Nothing about Amyjane's life led to her murder. That was a decision beyond her control. Yet her life did, without question, make it harder for police *to* track down her killer, and that is something the community at large criticized the police over.

CHAPTER THIRTY-SIX

1. Pendleton Police Department press release, August 11, 2013. NBC, KNDO/KNDU.

2. "DNA Found after Pendleton Assault Linked to 2012 Slaying." *Tri-City Herald*, August 20, 2013.

CHAPTER THIRTY-SEVEN

1. Cockle, Richard. "Pendleton murder, assault suspect was 'having a Coke . . . as calm as if he owned the place.'" *The Oregonian*, August 29, 2013.

2. Wright, Phil. "Wanted Man Captured at the Convention Center," *East Oregonian*, August 28, 2013.

CHAPTER THIRTY-EIGHT

1. All interview video was provided by Pendleton Police Department following a FOIA request. The interview, conducted over several hours the night Luke was arrested, included his confession. August 28, 2013.

CHAPTER THIRTY-NINE

1. Galatians 5: 22-23. New International Version, Bible.

2. Ioana, Illie. "No One is Born a Serial Killer." *Procedia* - Social and Behavioral Sciences, 2013.

3. Sharma, Meher. *The Development of Serial Killers: A Grounded Theory Study.* Eastern Illinois University, 2018.

4. Cyranoski, David. "What CRISPR-baby Prison Sentences May Mean for Research." *Nature,* January 3, 2020.

5. Powel, Alvin. "CRISPR's Breakthrough Technology" The Harvard Gazette, 16 May 2018.

6. Cohen, Jon. "CRISPR, the revolutionary genetic 'scissors' honored by Chemistry Nobel," *Science Magazine,* Oct.7, 2020.

7. Park, Alice. "Experts are calling for a Ban on Gene Editing of Human Embryos." Time Magazine, 13 March 2019.

8. Schmiz, Ron. "Gene-editing scientist's actions are a product of Modern China." *National Public Radio,* 5 Feb. 2019.

9. Regaldo, Antonia. "Chinese scientists are creating CRISPR babies." MIT Technology Review, 25 Nov. 2018.

10. Funk, Cary; Hefferon, Meg. "Public Views of Gene Editing for Babies depend on how it would be used." Pew Research Center, July 2018.

CHAPTER FORTY

1. Beaver, Kevin, Dr. Florida State University. Interviews by phone and correspondence.

2. Hogenboom, Melissa. "Two Genes Linked with Violent Crime." *BBC News*, Oct. 28, 2014.

3. Rogers, Stephen. "Warrior Gene linked to Violent Crime." *Irish Times*, 29 Oct. 2014.

4. Frazier, Annabelle et al. "Born this way? A review of neurobiological and environmental evidence for the etiology of psychopathy." *Personality neuroscience vol. 2 e8. 23 Oct. 2019.*

5. Anderson, Nathaniel E, and Kent A Kiehl. "Psychopathy: developmental perspectives and their implications for treatment." *Restorative neurology and neuroscience vol. 32,1 2014.*

6. Keeland, Kate. "Study finds psychopaths have distinct brain structure." *Reuters,* May 7, 2012.

7. Butterfield, Fox. "When Crime is a Family Affair." *The Atlantic,* Oct.20, 2018.

ADDITIONAL RESOURCES
THAT INFORMED THIS WORK

Butterfield, Fox. *In My Father's House: A New View of How Crime Runs in Families*. New York City, NY: Alfred A. Knopf, 2018.

Hallman, Tom. "Pendleton Victim's Husband Looks to the Future." *The Oregonian*, 29 August 2013.

J. Craig Venter Institute. "Archibald E. Garrod postulates that genetic defects cause many inherited diseases." *Genome News Network* 200-2004. <www.genomenewsnetwork.org/resources/timeline/1908_Garrod.php>.

Leavitt, Sarah A. *Deciphering the Genetic Code*. 2010. <https://history.nih.gov/display/history/Nirenberg+History+-+Gregor+Mendel>.

Maddox, Brenda. *Rosalind Franklin: The Dark Lady of DNA by Brenda Maddox*. New York City: Harper Perennial, 2003.

Oubré, Alondra. "The Extreme Warrior Gene: A Reality Check." *Scientia Salon* 7/2/2015. <https://scientiasalon.wordpress.com/2014/07/31/the-extreme-warrior-gene-a-reality-check/>.

Parshley, Lois. *Can Genes Make you Kill? Popular Science.* 28 April 2016. < https://www.popsci.com/can-your-genes-make-you-kill>.

Reuell, Peter. "The Genetics of Regeneration." *The Harvard Gazette,* 2019.

Richardson, Sarah. "A Violence in the Blood." *Discover Magazine,* October 1993: 30-33. <https://www.discovermagazine.com/the-sciences/a-violence-in-the-blood>.

Rickert, Tom. "Woman's Hobby May Have Led to Her Harm." *Waukesha Daily Freeman,* 6th August 1973.

Springstead, Douglas. *Lincoln Case* Zacharias. 2020. phone call, correspondence with Doug Spingstead.

State of Michigan vs. Gene D. Lincoln. Baraga County, Michigan. 1973.

State of Michigan vs. Gene D. Lincoln. Baraga County. 1973. Court Testiomny from Gene Lincoln.

Vevera, Dr. Jan, et. al. ""Rare Copy Number Variation in Extremely Impulsively Violent Males." *Genes, Brain and Behavior,* 2019.

Wright, Phil. "Chief Clears Up Rumors About Slaying." *East Oregonian,* 28 August 2012.

"Wide Search for City Woman Fails." *Waukesha Daily Freeman* n.d.: 1973.

Yuming, Yang and Xue Jiru. *Bamboo resources and their utilization in China.* n.d. Bioversity International, Southwest Foresty College. <https://www.bioversityinternational.org/fileadmin/bioversity/publications/Web_version/572/ch10.htm>.